Hot Rods
Roadsters ▪ Coupes ▪ Customs

Dain Gingerelli

motorbooks

First published in 2009 by Motorbooks, an imprint of MBI Publishing Company, 400 First Avenue North, Suite 300, Minneapolis, MN 55401 USA

Motorbooks titles are also available at discounts in bulk quantity for industrial or sales-promotional use. For details write to Special Sales Manager at MBI Publishing Company, 400 First Avenue North, Suite 300, Minneapolis, MN 55401 USA.

To find out more about our books, visit us online at www.motorbooks.com.

Library of Congress Cataloging-in-Publication Data

Gingerelli, Dain, 1949–
 Hot rods : roadsters, coupes, customs / Dain Gingerelli.
   p. cm.
 ISBN 978-0-7603-3516-1 (pbk. : alk. paper)
 1. Hot rods. 2. Automobiles, Home-built. I. Title.
 TL236.3.G562 2009
 629.28'786—dc22

                    2008044298

Editor: Melinda Keefe
Designer: LK Design Inc., Laura Rades

Printed in Singapore

About the Author:
Dain Gingerelli is a well-known automotive journalist whose work has appeared in magazines like *Street Rodder*, *Rod & Custom*, *Old Skool Rodz*, and *Motor Trend*. He has written several books on hot rods for Motorbooks, including *Ford Hot Rods*, *Hot Rod Milestones*, and *Hot Rod Roots*. He lives in Mission Viejo, California.

Contents

Introduction

Among the more profound comments I've heard about hot rod styling was one that came from car builder Pete "P-Wood" Eastwood. Pete has built, or helped build, some landmark hot rods during the past few decades, so I've always respected his judgment about cars. The year was 1995, and Pete and I were standing near the entrance to the Mid-Winter Rod Run at Hemet, California, Airport, lazily entertaining ourselves watching cars roll in for the day. Had a bystander not known better he or she probably would have thought that Pete and I were the show judges, sizing up the contestants for the day. Finally, one car passed in front of us, and a less articulate person would have thought its owner had been on drugs when building this hot rod—that or the owner had been terribly abused as a child and had taken out his or her frustrations on the car. In any case, as the hot rod motored by, Pete gave it a hard look before casually commenting in his familiar nonchalant tone, "How can somebody get something that's so easy, so wrong?"

P-Wood had a point, and although his comment amused me at the time, he had, in effect, nailed down in a single sentence the whole concept of what hot rod styling is all about. Indeed, as a motojournalist who has penned several hot rod books and worked for two major hot rod magazines since 1972, I've seen tens of thousands of hot rods, and truth be told, a large portion of their builders got something that was— to borrow P-Wood's words—"so easy, so wrong." That's not to say that every hot rodder blunders through a build, because I've been in shops and garages where some very talented guys magically transformed rusted old hulks into sparkling show-stopping hot rods. Even so, there remains a small army of hot rodders at rod runs, cruise nights, and car shows across the country that hasn't fully grasped, or doesn't have a thorough understanding of, the concept that a well-planned theme gives the car unity and, well, *style.*

More than once, I've seen owners stumble through builds, mixing one styling element with another. The results can be catastrophic, usually a car that's an amalgamation of parts that, while stylish in their own right, don't blend with one another in the final build. I'm not talking about styling features like wood floorboards or taped-on chrome; those are simply wrong components for the wrong thing. Instead, I'm addressing builders

1 Body styles make all the difference. The 1940 Willys coupe has always been a favorite for the Pro Street look.

who view each component on a car as its own single entity. By doing this, they fail to perceive the big picture, which contains *all* the parts, and how all those parts play upon one another to give the hot rod panache, even personality—or, in a word, *style*.

The parts selection process can't begin until you actually have a car or pickup truck you intend to convert into a hot rod. For the most part, this book will deal with traditional-style hot rods, a styling theme that many hot rod builders throughout time have considered to represent an enduring look. Although any brand of car can be built using traditional styling methods, the marque that has prevailed among hot rodders throughout the decades is Ford.

Indeed, there's no arguing that early Fords make excellent platforms for hot rods. They still are plentiful in number, affordable in price, and compact in size, making them ideal for modifying. They've been that way since practically the beginning, too, when young men back in the 1920s and 1930s modified their Model T Fords to go fast. Soon modified Fords, especially Model Ts, Model As, and 1932 models, could be found in vast numbers competing on the crusty, alkaline-baked dry lakebeds of Southern California and on gritty oval dirt tracks throughout America. They raced on serpentine road courses, too, and perhaps the most notable was Mines Field (1932–1936), a B-shaped course traversing land

2

that eventually became consumed by Los Angeles International Airport.

Fittingly, then, most of the cars in this book are based on early Fords, specifically Model T (1908–1927), Model A (1928–1931), Model B (1932 or "Deuce"), Model 40 (1933–1934), and what have become known as "fat fendereds" (1935–1948). We'll also look at a few Fords from later years, just to show that not all Ford hot rods are from the pre–World War II days, and I've included various non-Ford hot rods, again to help illustrate that any car is worthy of becoming a hot rod if the builder does his or her homework during the building process.

It's also worth noting that even though some Ford car bodies

and frames are nearly 100 years old, today's hot rod aftermarket is rife with reproduction parts, giving hot rodders the option of constructing their cars from all-new components, or mix-matching them with original inventory. Perhaps the most popular reproduction body style in either fiberglass or metal is the Deuce roadster. More than once I've heard a hot rodder state: "There are probably more 1932 Ford roadsters today than when Henry built them back in 1932." Truth be told, Henry Ford originally built less than 1,000 roadsters, so do the math to see if that statement holds water.

This begs the question: Are these reproduction (re-pop) hot rods really hot rods? If they

2 Black paint, traditional flames, a Moon Equip pressure tank, and American mag wheels set the tempo for this hot rod.

3 A car's stance has a lot to do with its style. This 1932 Ford coupe sits low thanks to its classic dropped front axle.

embody the spirit of what started this form of automotive culture in the first place, I say, yes. Like their predecessors, these scratch-built hot rods are light in weight, are minimalist in design, and reflect the attitudes and personalities of their builders. So, whether a hot rod is based on an original body and frame or utilizes reproduction parts, if it looks like a hot rod, sounds like a hot rod, and goes fast like a hot rod, then it must be a hot rod.

The following pages include photos of what I consider to be some of the top traditional-style Ford hot rods that I've photographed during the past 20 years. I've included a few nontraditional cars, too, and as

stated previously, you'll find some later-model cars from Dearborn and Detroit in the mix to illustrate that not all hot rods are necessarily based on old Ford tin. I hope you have as much fun reading this book as I had putting it together. The time spent gathering the images allowed me the opportunity to view color transparencies that I had all but forgotten about. In the end I realized just how wonderful this hobby can be, and how talented some of its people are with the tools they have to work with in their garages and shops. Those builders are my heroes—and that even includes those builders who got it wrong.

1

Body Types and Styles:
Roadsters, Convertibles, Phaetons, and Cabriolets

1 Bill Nielsen's 1927 Ford is a classic example of a roadster modified for racing at the Southern California dry lakes. The body is based on the front half of a 1927 Ford Phaeton. It was cut in half and then narrowed by 8 inches.

You can't have a hot rod project unless you have a car. This first section is devoted to the various body types and styles of cars available for hot rodding. If you ask some hot rodders about what car is best for hot rodding, though, they'll tell you there's only one body style, and that's a Ford roadster.

By definition a roadster is a two-seat, open-top car that doesn't have roll-up side windows. Even though original Ford roadsters came from Dearborn with removable side curtains to help keep out the elements, you won't find many hot rodders today encumbering their cars with those frugal amenities. We can make concessions for rumble seats, which, in effect, give a roadster the advantage of carrying two more passengers.

As an aside, convertibles and cabriolets are similar to roadsters, but they have roll-up side windows. That's a very basic distinction, and for the record, Ford began giving its roadsters (not to be confused with its Sport Coupe models) roll-up windows in 1935, although as late as 1936 the Dearborn company still produced true roadsters. Phaetons are another open-top model and have front and rear seating.

Finally, we can separate hot rod roadsters into their own classifications, among them: highboy, lowboy, T-bucket, track-T, lakester, and full-fendered. This chapter will showcase each of these styles, so let's dispense with the words and get on with checking out some styling ideas for hot rod roadsters, convertibles, cabriolets, and phaetons.

2 Want funk? Jim "Jake" Jacobs' 1928 Model A offers it in spades. He and a group of friends painted the phaeton by hand, and later Jake used pages from old hot rod magazines to form a rolling decoupage.

3 In 1950, Bill Neikamp's 1929 Ford was presented the first-ever America's Most Beautiful Roadster (AMBR) trophy at the Oakland Roadster Show. The blue roadster's timeless beauty remains unsurpassed.

4 Manny Betes built this car in 1939, and the highboy remained in its original "hot rod" condition the day I photographed it in 1993. He formed the hood from surplus aircraft sheet aluminum.

5 Here's another former AMBR winner. George Krikorian's lowboy 1929 Ford won the prestigious 6-foot trophy in 1960. The car retains its original candy-red lacquer and pearl-white upholstery.

6 Joe Scanlin's 1929 Ford illustrates just how powerful the simplistic beauty of a highboy can be. The all-steel, original body is set on 1932 Ford frame rails, a common combination for this body and frame.

7 You're looking at a combined hot rod history of more than 180 years! All three roadsters were built before World War II. That's Ed Iskenderian's legendary T on the left, John Athan's "Elvis Car" Model A in the middle, and Tom Leonardo Sr.'s 1929—originally built by Herman Leham—to the right.

8

9

10

11

12

8   Some kids never grow up! That's John Athan behind the wheel of his "Elvis Car," the 1929 Ford that Elvis Presley drove in the movie *Loving You.* Ed Iskenderian is riding shotgun.

9   When John Athan built his A V-8 highboy in 1940, he used the rear window from a new Chrysler for the windshield. Tom Leonardo restored the car, including the windshield frame, in 1997.

10   This is a prime example of what a traditional A V-8 looks like. The name derives from the body and engine—it's a Model A equipped with a Ford V-8 flathead.

11   Hot rods are supposed to be fun! Steve Wickert stuck to that formula when he cut the roof off a Model A sedan to create this phantom phaeton.

12   Who says building a hot rod is expensive? Tommy Leonardo Jr. grabbed a few spare parts from his father's inventory to build this 1931 Ford lowboy for less than $1,000.

13 Ron Bertrum's T-bucket is based on an early—probably 1960s vintage—Cal Automotive fiberglass body. The drivetrain is early Ford, too, with a 1948 engine, 1939 transmission, and 1948 rear end.

14 Not all Ford hot rods are black. Gary Moline selected a late-model Chevrolet blue, doused it with traditional-style flames, and then set the package on Halibrand wheels with BFGoodrich radial tires.

15 Okay, it's time to get funky! This 1941 Buick convertible served as the platform for a rather nice and different kind of hot rod. The painted grille complements the rolled front pan.

16 This is one of my all-time favorite cars that I have photographed. The 1936 Ford Phaeton was originally modified back in the 1970s and has most recently been restored by Gary Vahling in Colorado.

17 Morgwn Pennypacker mounted a cut-down cab from a 1937 Dodge truck onto a 1930 Ford frame to create this channeled lowboy hot rod.

13

14

15

16

17

18

19

20

21

22

18   One of the first-ever T-buckets, Tommy "TV" Ivo's 1923 Ford looks much like it did when he built it in the mid-1950s. Its Buick engine is fed by an early Hilborn fuel injection system.

19   Restoration and hot rod specialist Dave Crouse built Jim Tuggle's 1929 Ford, painting it Dodge Viper Red. The interior has all-leather upholstery and wool carpet.

20   Less is more, and in this case, less paint means more patina. Jeff Nichols located this 1932 Ford in a Midwest barn, scraped off a few barnacles, gave the flathead engine a quick tune-up, and then hit the road.

21   Here's a great example of a 1938 Ford Convertible Deluxe. Hal Peterson's metallic blue custom has its windshield chopped 2 inches, and for additional style there's a sunken license plate and classic flipper wheel covers.

22   Built back in the early 1950s, the Joe Nitti roadster is considered a landmark hot rod. David Zivot located the car and had Dave Crouse restore it in time to win the Bruce Meyer Preservation Award at the 2000 Oakland Roadster Show.

23 I photographed Jim Richardson's 1929 full-fendered Model A in 1997, and the car's simplistic beauty remains just as captivating to me now. I especially like its Model B (1932) four-cylinder engine fed by two Stromberg 97 carbs.

24 You'll see many variations for T-buckets, but one of the cleanest I've photographed is Homer Overton's, which is based on a 1923 Ford body. I consider its rear frame member and suspension especially clean.

25 Lyle and Sherry Penfold's 1940 Mercury convertible has all the styling touches associated with a traditional custom. Moreover, it was built by a man who understands custom cars—Terry Hegman.

26 Todd Gold cut down a 1930 Ford Tudor Sedan to make this phaeton hot rod. To give the car its own panache, he even left the bullet hole that someone put in its right rear quarter panel years ago.

27 When it comes to showing off its stylish silhouette, few hot rods can top Mark Morton's 1929 Ford. It draws the eye from any angle, and I used this car as the lead photo for the final chapter in my *Ford Hot Rods* book.

23

24

25

26

27

28

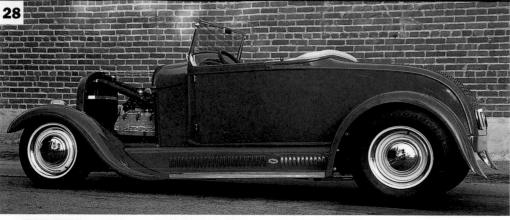

29

30

31

32

33

28 A hot rod's stance is important, and Butch Phillips gave his 1929 Ford the right stance. The big-little tire combination includes 145/60-15 front and 235/70-15 rear tires on early Ford wheels.

29 This A V-8 is a survivor from the 1950s. Known as the "Racer Brown Car," the all-steel Model A has a buggy spring rear suspension with an early Ford rear end and 1939 Ford taillights.

30 Here's another hot rod that proves you don't need a big budget to succeed. Dave Stalhler was in high school when he built this T-bucket. He accumulated most of the parts while shopping at swap meets.

31 Want something different? Do as Joe Graffio did; he located the race car he originally built in the late 1940s, restored it, and then parked it alongside his Harwood-body Deuce roadster he built in 2001. I snapped this picture in 2002.

32 Harold Johanson was 16 years old when he bought this Model A in 1944. The car sports 16-inch tires, 1939 Lincoln hydraulic brakes, a 1933 Model C four-cylinder engine with two-port Riley head, and a 1956 Ford truck steering box.

33 When I spotted Howard Holiman's 1927 Ford modified roadster at a cruise night back in 1993, I felt as though I had drifted back in time. He bought the narrowed body at the 1990 L.A. Roadster Show swap meet.

34 Dennis Love called on Martin Williams to build this traditional-style hot rod. The California Custom Roadster (CCR) fiberglass body is highlighted by various, and original, Ford components. I especially like the louvers on the Model A frame rails.

35 In 1999 I photographed all the Deacons Kar Klub members' cars in San Diego's old district. I especially liked Rod Roder's chopped (literally) 1956 Ford Fairlane Victoria. How low can you go?

36 Looking to build a 1970s-era T-bucket? Then you need to study Dan Woods' style. This original, based on a 1917 Ford body and built three decades ago by Woods, is currently owned by hot rod icon Blackie Gejeian.

37 Jonny Guilmet II considers himself and his Deacons club members to be "original" hot rodders, meaning their cars are built in the spirit of the 1950s. His 1929 Ford roadster pickup makes a strong statement to that order.

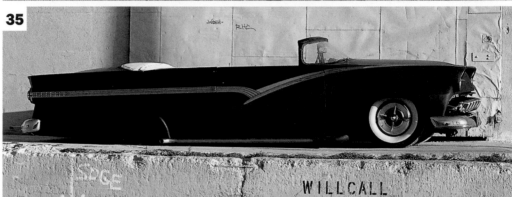

38

39

40

38 Not a roadster and not a coupe, Mike Welch's hot rod is based on a 1932 Ford Cabriolet. It was a racer in the 1950s, and Mike said the body required extensive work to return it to this condition. I photographed it in 1998.

39 Scott DePron's 1932 highboy was built to commemorate his grandfather's participation in the Gilmore races held in Los Angeles back in the mid-1930s. The wheels are authentic magnesium, and check out the leather hood strap.

40 Another timeless hot rod I photographed belonged to Lewis Wolff. He built this Deuce roadster back in 1962. Its silver-based candy-red paint job was applied at that time, too, and it remains in pristine condition today.

41 The modifications on Ted Fisher's 1936 Ford are so subtle that it almost takes my breath away. He chopped the windshield and top, and lowered it ever so slightly.

42 Some people say that black hot rods are a dime a dozen. Maybe, but Don Mathis used just the right amount of white, coupled with red stripes and accent colors, to make his 1934 Ford stand out from the others.

43 I'm also a motorcycle guy, so I couldn't help but slip in this matching hot rod and custom motorcycle. Both were built by Rucker Performance, but for different customers.

44

45

46

44 When Ed Iskenderian's legendary T-roadster was on exhibit at the Wally Parks National Hot Rod Association (NHRA) Motorsports Museum, I rolled it outside for a few photos for my "Milestone" feature in *Street Rodder Magazine*. If you need an explanation about this car, you just don't know much about hot rod history.

45 One of the more colorful characters I've met through the years is Gabby Garrison. He was a hot rodder back in the 1930s, and since then he hadn't changed when I photographed his tribute T in 1997. The car was based on a hot rod he built back in the 1930s when he was a high school student in Long Beach, California.

46 Gary Vahling is a builder who has "the touch." Whatever he builds just seems to shine in every category, and this 1936 Ford phaeton is no exception. While not a traditional car, it's traditional in the sense that it's a hot rod, and that's good enough for me.

47 This 1927 T-roadster has been rebuilt and altered since Dick Williams won the AMBR award with it in 1954, but it still has a timeless beauty about it. It's part of Blackie Gejeian's collection today.

48 This Model T hot rod appeared as the first car in my book *Hot Rod Milestones* (later re-titled *The Hot Rod*). It belongs to Hank Becker, who drives it often. The Model T went 80 miles per hour at the drags. I was especially honored that Hank allowed me time behind the old wooden steering wheel after our photo session.

49 When I photographed Frank Mack's T back in 1992, it was probably the first time his car had been out of the garage in years. His 1926 Ford earned the top award at the first–ever Detroit Autorama in 1953. Bruce Meyer bought the car after he saw my pictures in the November 1992 issue of *American Rodder* magazine.

Body Types and Styles:
Coupes

When the Southern California Timing Association (SCTA) was formed in 1937 to regulate racing on the dry lakebeds, the rules applied only to roadsters. At the time, hot rodders didn't consider closed-top cars, including two-seater coupes, to be worthy candidates for hot rods. Consequently, the early days of SCTA dry lakes racing was limited to roadsters and modified streamliners. Later, organizations like the Rusetta Timing Association filled the void, recognizing coupes as well as roadsters at their events, and eventually the SCTA acquiesced to the closed-top crowd, too.

Despite such a shaky beginning, coupes have always been prime candidates for converting into hot rods. Like the roadsters, coupes can be modified to become highboys, lowboys, full-fendereds, and everything in between.

Furthermore, like the roadsters, the most favored model coupe is the 1932 Ford. Model A coupes—the 1928–1931 model years—look similar to the Deuce coupe, which accounts for their high stature on the rodding totem pole. But we're not here to choose family favorites; we're here to look at some cool hot rods. Here then, and in no particular order, are what I consider prime examples of hot rod coupes.

2 The raw-edge lines of a typical rat rod become obvious with Julio Hernandez's chopped (7 inches) and channeled (7¾ inches) Model A. The car has a 1953 Merc V-8 linked to a 1962 Mustang rear end via a 1939 Ford transmission. I photographed this car in Old Town San Diego where the Padres' baseball stadium now stands.

3 Gary Moline started with a complete 1937 Ford to build this hot rod. "I paid through the nose for this thing," he told me. "It was junk, but it was complete." He painted it 1990 Ford T-Bird red and gave it an all-white Naugahyde interior.

4 Want real old school? Check out Dave Crouse's five-window Deuce. Dave specializes in restoring hot rods, and he's brought back some rather famous cars to the circuit. His personal 1932 is rather subdued and is all steel. It still has its flathead V-8 for power, too.

2

3

4

5

6

7

5 John Vanderhaar's 1930 Ford looks like a typical car you'd see cruising the local burger stand back in 1962. I especially like the Olds Fiesta tri-spinner wheel covers with wide-whitewall tires. The stock frame rails are boxed for strength, in old-school fashion.

6 I photographed Dave and Betty Luethe's 1934 Ford five-window during the Bonneville National's 50th anniversary meet. I'm not a big fan of two-tone paint, but the colors on this car were compelling enough for me to single it out. The car could sit a little lower in the back end, but I'll take it!

7 Hot rods are supposed to have attitude, and Craig Elderson's 1931 Ford has it in spades. The top is chopped 5 inches, the rumble seat's lid is covered with louvers, and the lakes pipes along the sides emit a really nice burble from the overbored Chevy 383 engine.

8 Doug Kenny traded a year-old Cadillac in 1977 for this chopped (2½ inches) 1934 five-window. The car had been a hot rod for a number of years already before Doug freshened it up with black lacquer paint and a maroon-and-ivory rolled-and-pleated interior.

9 John Walker called on Dave Crouse to rodify his 1932 five-window. The bodywork includes graduated louvers around the hood blisters that were formed to clear the 331-cubic-inch Chrysler Hemi engine's valve covers. The rear wheels are authentic Halibrand mags.

10 You can't miss Ron Drezek's highboy 1932 five-window at a rod run. The checkered-flag graphics along the hood panels, cowl, and doors make it stand out, even though it has the same black paint as many other hot rods.

8

9

10

11 This car can give you an idea of how tire technology has improved over the years. When Lewis Wolff built his 1932 three-window in the 1960s, he said the Goodyear H75-15 tires were "the widest tire I could get at the time." I photographed the car in 1992.

12 Jimmy Houston complemented the Passion Red paint on his 1932 Ford highboy with the right amount of decals, pinstripes, and cowl graphics to make you look twice. The top is chopped (2½ inches) and filled, and the hood carries enough louvers to maintain the theme.

13 The owner of this full-fendered 1932 five-window had owned his car for 30 years before giving it a facelift shortly before the National Street Rod Association's (NSRA) annual nationals meet, held in Louisville, Kentucky, in 2000. I especially enjoy the car's simplistic beauty accented with 1960s-style pinstriping.

14 When I attended the 1990 NSRA nationals in Columbus, Ohio, for *American Rodder* magazine, I was assigned a story about the "ugly cars"—that is, non-Fords. I found this 1937 Dodge that had its fenders stripped, its top chopped (not sure how much), and a rebuilt Mopar 383 engine placed under its louvered hood. I like this car.

15 Here's another example of less being more. Wayne Hartman performed all the bodywork for his 1932 five-window. He told me an experienced bodyman coached him. Black paint will reveal flaws in the bodywork, and when I photographed this car in 1997 there were no flaws to be found. Wayne had one heck of a coach.

16 I had a fun time photographing Hal Rasberry's 1941 Willys coupe. The paint job bristled with color, those big meats under the rear fenders beckoned for some close-ups, and the supercharger sticking out of the hood always gave me something to focus on.

17 You can't help but warm up to Mike Armstrong's 1931 Ford. A dropped I-beam front axle lowers the car—as you can see here—into the weeds, and I personally like the leather hood straps. Under that hood sits a Model B four-cylinder engine with Cragar head and two Stromberg 81 carbs.

DRIVERS

Hot rods are meant to be driven. It's as simple as that. Anything less is considered, by many diehard hot rodders anyway, to be a trailer queen or a show car, or both.

I subscribe to the belief that hot rods are to be driven, and so I've included just a few of the many drivers that I have had the privilege to photograph. Think of these as real-world cars for real-world rodders.

The daily commute for Gary Moline was the fun part of his workday when he owned this 1932 Ford three-window that was based on a Total Cost Involved (TCI) chassis and Gibbons fiberglass body. This photo was taken on Glendora Mountain Road.

I had the opportunity to ride in Russ Tilkes' 1929 Ford Tudor, and it was tight as a drum. It was also fast, turning 12-second quarter-mile times. Russ drove this car to countless rod runs from his shop in Golden, Colorado.

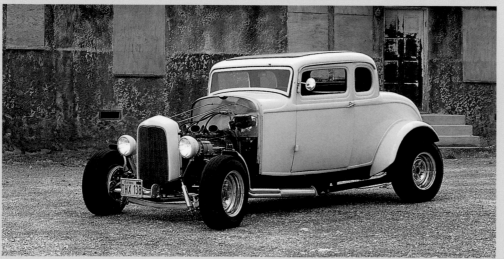

Okay, so owner Rick Figari doesn't drive the *American Graffiti* coupe much these days. Still, I had to include it here because it is perhaps the most famous cruising car of all time, thanks to the movie's plot that saw actor Paul Le Mat behind the wheel.

I'm not sure how many times Jake Jacobs drove his fenderless 1934 Ford across the country, but each trip brought with it a new adventure. Jake never let anything stand in the way of a good ride.

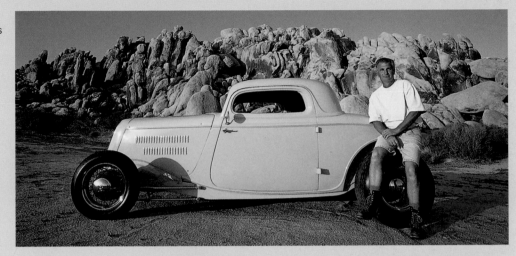

Tom Leonardo bought his 1930 Ford back in the mid-1960s when he was about 12 years old. He's been driving it ever since, and I had the privilege of riding with him at the inaugural River City Reliability Run in 1995.

Speaking of the River City Reliability Run, here's a shot of some cars heading down (up?) the Rim of the World Highway in the San Bernardino Mountains. Mark Morton sponsors this run that's open only to hot rods favoring pre-1955 styling.

Body Types and Styles:
Sedans and Woodies

In 1965 a high school friend of mine, Jeff, bought a roadworthy 1949 Ford woodie for a few hundred bucks. Jeff was a surfer, and back then about the only people who really warmed up to the wood wagons were surfers. That was then, but this is now, and it seems that today everybody enjoys the old timber trolleys. Present-day hot rodders also enjoy woodie sedans, specifically two-doors that look sporty and accommodate at least twice the number of occupants as coupes or roadsters.

Unlike the previous chapters that focused on pre-1950 cars, these pages include later-model sedans. For good reason, too: sedans from the 1950s and 1960s make great hot rods. Complete door-slammers are available for affordable prices, and if you shop carefully, you can buy a car that requires little in the way of parts replacement. I know because my daily driver is a 1964 Chevy II Nova that I purchased complete and ready to restore. Its six-cylinder engine had 39,800 original miles on it, and for the most part, the chassis was as tight as the day it rolled off the assembly line. The car's chrome and stainless-steel parts were straight, and the AM radio even worked!

So when you look at the later-model cars in this chapter, don't do so with envy. Look with the knowledge that you, too, can build your own hot rod for half the price you could pay for a new jelly-bean car that auto companies offer today.

2 If you own a woodie restoration business, you had better own a woodie wagon! Doug and Suzy Carr, of Wood 'n Carr, let me photograph their 1951 Ford next to the ocean at Long Beach, just a stone's throw from their shop in Signal Hill, California.

3 The sun is going down, the surf behind you lazily washes up on shore while the tide comes in, and you're done for the day. Outside your beach house sits your woodie. Well, that's the life we envision for Alan and Lana Lundgren's 1936 Ford wagon, anyway.

4 Curiosity killed the cat, so the tuxedoed cat sniffing Dave Petersen's 1940 Ford Tudor better be careful! Where the cat is, you would eventually find a Super Bell disc brake kit and new tie rods linked to a Magnum 4-inch dropped axle.

5 What a difference a year makes. While most rodders enjoy the 1940 Ford, few have warmed up to the 1941 model year, but Sal Tijerina's 1941 is clean and well stated, shown here at a winery in Ontario, California. I think the car's Laramie Beige color works well in this setting.

6 Time to put on the blue bowtie and check out Ron Russell's 1937 Chevrolet. The chassis has a Mustang II front suspension kit, and the rear rides on a Chassis Engineering setup. The American Racing Torq-Thrust wheels do a nice job of maintaining the subtlety while telling you this is a hot rod.

2

3

4

5

6

7 Danny Osburn actually wanted a 1958 Chevrolet Impala before he bought this 1958 Bel Air "for a low, ridiculous price." My first-ever car was a 1958 Chevy Biscayne four-door that I shared with my brother. It didn't look anything like Danny's custom, but my brother and I still loved that old five-eight.

8 Rods and customs aren't supposed to have four doors, but we'll make an exception with Richard Graves' 1958 Cadillac Eldorado. The hood and trunk were shaved in the usual custom-car manner.

9 Pink? Well, actually it's called Sandstone Coral, and Gary Moline chose that color, along with Colonial White, to set the tone for his 1956 Ford post sedan that has a 390–inch Ford V-8 fed by dual-quad Holley carburetors. He took me for a ride in the "Mary Kay Car," as we affectionately called it, and it was fast!

10 Through the years, I have photographed all of Gary Moline's hot rods, but this one was the first. The 1956 Oldsmobile is lowered, has reversed chrome rims with baby moons, and is powered by a 371-inch, 312-horsepower J-2 engine with three carburetors.

11   Denver's outlying industrial area served as a great backdrop for Jim Ross' 1957 Oldsmobile, which has an all-white interior with a J-2 engine package. I like the painted reversed wheels with narrow whitewall tires.

12   Suzy Proche describes her 1957 Ford hardtop as a mild custom. The hood and trunk emblems have been shaved, custom grille tubes were put in place, and the car sits slightly lower in the back, according to the style of the 1950s and 1960s.

13   To help emphasize the 1955 DeSoto's long lines, Glenn Matejzel and his father, Bob Matejzel, left the original stainless-steel trim along the beltline and gave the hood and trunk a quick shave. The checker-painted Lancer wheel covers accent the wild purple and cream paint.

14   Here's another Deacons Kar Klub car, Jonny Guilmet's 1956 Oldsmobile two-door post. He painted it with lacquers using flattening agents. Who would have thought that the red trim in the wheel covers would look so cool alongside purple?

15 Tom Roth chose an interesting car for his hot rod project—a 1922 Ford Model T center-door sedan. The door is placed in the middle of the body, behind the driver's seat and in front of the passenger's seat.

16 I was really lucky to locate the late "Lil' John" Buttera's landmark 1926 Ford Model T sedan to feature in my *Hot Rod Milestones* book, published in 1998. Mike Sweeny owned the car and drove it everywhere. He said the old T was as tight then as it was when John built it in 1974.

17 Money is generally a consideration among rodders, so Joe Haska kept his investment minimal with his 1946 Ford Tudor. He bought the car—complete and running—for about $5,000, then invested another five grand to bring it to the level you see here. Yes, hot rods can be affordable.

18 Few people want to chop the top of a station wagon or panel delivery, but 3 inches were taken off the top of Tom Lindemann's 1956 Chevrolet Sedan Delivery. As the license plate states: WUT A CUT (what a cut).

19 I caught Mike and Julie Scaplo on their family vacation when I photographed their 1931 Model A at the 1999 NSRA nationals. The top was chopped 3 inches, all body seams were filled, the rear pan was rolled, rear fenders were bobbed 3 inches, and a 1932 Ford radiator shell was added.

20 One of the most famous hot rods of all time is Bob McCoy's 1940 Ford, built in the late 1950s. Dave Kinnaman liked the car so much that he built his own. I caught up with him at the 2000 NSRA nationals to photograph it for *American Rodder* magazine.

21 The best way to show off a Ford Victoria sedan is with a full-side shot. I love the model's abbreviated rear window and sloping trunk section. It's a design that looks elegant, even if it is a bit snotty. This 1931 "Vicky" belongs to Jim Ver Duft.

22 If you're a rat-rod fan, then you'll appreciate Joshua Shaw's 1932 Ford. Despite the highboy sedan's scruffy appearance, the car is in perfect mechanical condition. The drag slick tires aren't exactly street legal, and the drilled I-beam front axle is an appreciable throwback to the 1960s.

23 Don't be fooled by the primer finish; the sheet metal on David Julian's 1937 Ford sedan is smooth and ready for real paint, should he decide to do so. The yellow trim on the hubcap and the "Clay Smith Camshaft" decal on the lower front fender are nice touches.

20

21

22

23

The wooden floor in Wayne Cash's 1934 Ford pickup looks clean enough to eat off of! This angle shows just how well the fenders and running boards have been restored, too.

Body Types and Styles:
Trucks

Some people consider pickup trucks to be the toys of grownup boys. If they're talking about hot rod pickups, they wouldn't be far off in their assessment. Truth is, some of the coolest hot rods on the road *are* pickup trucks.

Rodifying a pickup truck isn't that much different than if you were to start with a roadster, coupe, or sedan. All body styles share the same essential mechanical components, except a truck also has the cargo bed to restore. Depending on the year of the truck, you can shorten the bed, straighten it to look new—or even better than new if you like—or cover it with a tonneau cover to retain the truck's versatility as a cargo hauler. Whatever you decide, you know that you can end up with a hot rod that offers all that you want—and more.

2 I saw Tom Leonardo Sr.'s 1936 Ford before he rebuilt it, and believe me, it looked nothing like this. Before the rebuild, he called the truck "Old Faithful." I kid him now by referring to it as "New Faithful."

3 Roadster pickups are cool because they mix two breeds into one. Jim Siegmund's 1929 Ford takes it one step further, using an old-school Model C four-cylinder engine with a Riley four-port head for power.

4 Warren "Hoke" Hokinson's 1935 Ford looks mild mannered, but under the hood is a 300-cubic-inch Ford flathead V-8. The rear end is based on a Columbia overdrive with 3.78:1 gears.

5 Roger Starkey engineered the air-shock rear suspension for his 1951 Chevrolet, and you can see the result here. The paint job consists of a green base coat mixed with black enamel.

6 At a glance, Mike and Cindy Armstrong's 1929 Ford looks rather unassuming, but the tachometer on the cowl sends a message. For further reading, go under the hood to see the Model B four-cylinder engine with a Cragar head and dual Stromberg 81 carburetors.

7 Martin Williams' 1936 Ford looks like it drove right out of 1959. I'm especially fond of the louvered hood, the wide whitewall tires, and the bed's white snap-on tonneau cover.

8 To give symmetry to his 1959 Ford F-100, Gary Moline matched the front and rear wheelwells, then filled them with red reversed wheels wrapped with Coker Classic tires. A 502-cubic-inch Ford V-8 sits under the hood.

9 Ford's classic Colonial White paint highlights Neil Giraldo's 1955 F-100. The truck was lowered several inches front and rear, and its classic five-spoke wheels were wrapped with contemporary radial tires.

10 After years of hauling miscellaneous hardware and cargo, this 1959 Ford's pickup bed was treated to some TLC. Considerable massaging resulted in the smooth floor you see here. The custom lock-box now hauls personal cargo.

11 The "Bob Jones Special" emblem on the tailgate was the final touch that Jim McNaul gave his 1953 F-100. Bob Jones owned a Ford dealership in Denver, Colorado, that built specials like this back in the 1950s.

12 A combination of stainless-steel slats and oak floor panels that have been stained and waxed finish off this pickup bed's floor. Careful what you put in there!

13 Who says you need a lot of chrome to make a hot rod pickup truck look cool? The grille on this Ford F-100 contains a mixture of chrome and gunmetal gray finish.

Body Treatments:
Taillights

1 One of the most distinct taillight treatments for a hot rod can be found on the 1960 Oakland Roadster Show winner, George Krikorian's "Emperor." The grille work he included does a nice job of tying both lights together.

Have you ever noticed that when you spot a hot rod, you generally view it first from the front? Even when you're at a rod run or cruise night, more than likely you position yourself so that your first take on the car is from the front, possibly so you can inspect the engine if it's a hoodless car or if its engine bonnet is propped open. After inspecting the engine, you make your way to view the interior. Only after you've completed those cursory examinations will you walk toward the car's hind section to see what's there.

That's too bad because some of a hot rod's best detail is found at the south end, where generally speaking, the taillights command the most attention. So, we're going to begin our look at specific hot rod ideas with the least-viewed area on the car. Grab your blinders and let's go look at some taillights.

2 Keep it simple, stupid. So this 1932 Ford retains its original taillight/license plate combination. The 1932 Olympics plaque is a nice touch.

3 The special rear pan with single-piece, flush-fit taillight accents the trimmed rear fenders on this Model A. The pan also conceals the rear suspension and offers an anchor for the dual exhausts.

4 Taillight lenses from the 1959 Cadillac are favorites for hot rodders. Those red-tip wonders fit neatly in the center of this 1957 Ford taillight.

5 Here's another example of cross-pollinating, this time affixing 1941 Chevrolet taillights to a 1932 Ford. The blue-dot centers have always been favored by rodders, although they're illegal in many states.

6 This isn't a third brake light; it's the only taillight on this modified roadster. Centering the taillight allows the builder to help show off the car's unique rear suspension.

7 The taillight assembly from a 1956 Mercury fits right inside the housing of a 1956 Ford's rear lights. Careful sizing like this may allow you to give the car a modified look without having to do metal work to get there!

8

9

10

11

12

8   A pair of inverted 1932 Ford taillights finish off the rear section of this 1923 Ford T-bucket. Some states offer historic license plates for hot rods.

9   Another example of mounting 1941 Chevrolet taillights is seen on this 1932 Ford coupe. These taillights are favored by rodders because they are simple and clean in design.

10   A classic tail section for an A V-8 Ford is seen here. The teardrop taillights are from a 1939 Ford. Dual exhausts, the transverse leaf spring, and a dropped crossmember also distinguish this car.

11   The historic license plate mounted in the original location on this 1932 model is simple yet eye catching. The blue-dot center and the pinstripes help identify this old car as a hot rod.

12   The round taillight lenses fit perfectly behind this handcrafted nerf bar. Also note how the bar's center crossmembers help frame the license plate.

13 Even though this 1929 Ford sedan has had its rear section modified and bumpers removed, the original Model A taillights help retain the car's original character.

14 Many old-car aficionados consider the 1936 Ford to be one of the Dearborn company's best designs. Contributing to its curvaceous lines are the taillights and stanchions.

15 Frenched taillights are popular on hot rods as well as custom cars. The 1959 Cadillac taillight lens looks like a missile ready to be fired from the tunneled housing on this Model A.

16 You can get creative with ordinary lights. This 1941 Chevrolet taillight is mounted vertically on a traditional A V-8 roadster.

17 A pristine prewar license plate, an antique club badge, and the original taillight give this 1932 Ford roadster the look of a hot rod from the early days.

Body Treatments:
Nerf Bars, Bumpers, Rolled Pans, and Gas Tanks

If there's one part of the car that automotive stylists the world over have trouble with, it's the bumper. Make that bumpers because you'll find these appendages on both ends of a car. Bumpers, those stylists might say, can be real bummers.

For years, though, hot rodders have come up with some rather unique and stylish solutions. One form of bumper that rodders have adapted for their cars is the bump bar used on oval-track racers and drag cars. Rodders often refer to

their adaptations as nerf bars, but the fact remains that their designs work by conforming to the styles of their cars.

Other refugees from the racetrack are gas tanks and auxiliary tanks. Dean Moon offered his spun-aluminum tanks as aftermarket items for racers, and today you can see these barrel-shaped fuel containers on all variations of hot rods. So, let's take a look and see what solutions some rodders have come up with regarding the front and rear sections of their cars.

2   What can you do with the frame horns of a 1932 Ford highboy roadster? Well, you can personalize it by fabricating the initial for your last name, as this builder did with the letter "G."

3   Strictly old-school here: the car club plaque is mounted to the front bumper, which also carries a custom center section.

4   This center push bar is a carryover from drag racing. The illuminated skull atop the bar serves as the hot rod's third brake light.

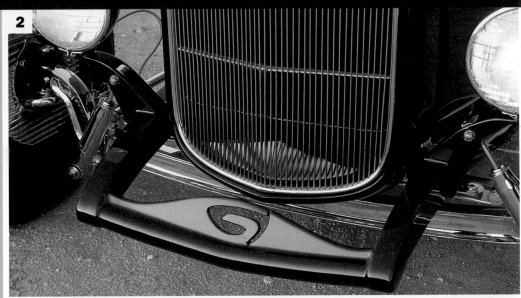

5 Nothing special here, but even so, the nerf bars, along with the truck grille insert, help give this 1934 Ford a special look. The pitted grille is an indication this car is being driven!

6 The teardrop taillight with blue-dot center helps make this 1938 Ford custom look, well, custom. The Early Ford V-8 Club of America club badge is a nice touch.

7 The Moon pressure tank and bright traditional flames on this Tom McMullen replica are today considered iconic styling features among hot rodders young and old.

8 Where to position the headlights in relation to the frame and radiator? Rob and Dave Crouse take measurements before mounting the familiar headlights to the Joe Nitti roadster.

9 Front nerf bars were first used on oval-track race cars. The bar on this A V-8 was built in 1940, when the car was converted into a hot rod.

10 The headlight placement on the Joe Nitti roadster is slightly higher than that of most cars. It is like no other arrangement found on a highboy roadster.

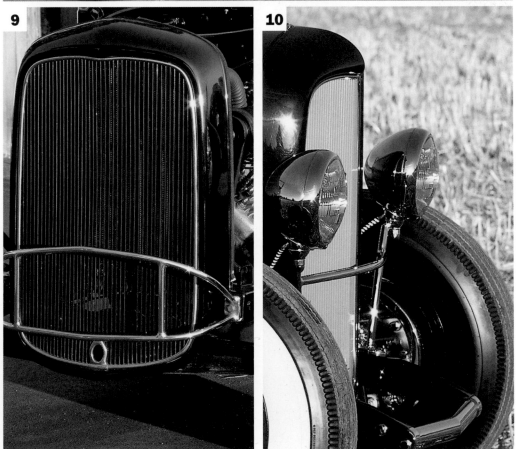

11 Remember, the number one rule about hot rodding is that there are no rules. That accounts for the wild artwork on this grille cover. You have to wonder if the engine overheats.

12 One of the most recognizable Ford Deuce hot rods is the Doane Spencer roadster. The front nerf bar and headlight placement is simple yet so direct and clean.

13 Remove the rear fender, roll the rear pan, French the license plate, tuck in a pair of exhaust tips, and this 1936 Ford Phaeton takes on a whole new look.

14   Recognize this front nerf bar? It was designed by Bob McCoy years ago when he built his original 1940 Ford Tudor. The painted grille slats are a nice touch.

15   Careful craftsmanship is what helped Bill Neikamp's 1929 Ford Model A V-8 win the first-ever AMBR award in 1950. The car's beauty is timeless.

16   The solitary gas cap on a Model A's cowl is so simple, yet so elegant. Savvy builders generally keep this distinguishing feature for their hot rods, too.

17   The decal on the gas tank of George Poteet's bobtail T gives the car a graceful look. I especially like the way the nerf bars are mounted so subtly to the frame's rails.

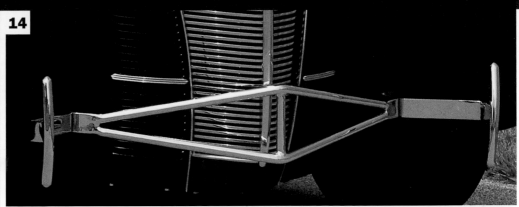

Body Treatments:
Grilles and Front Ornaments

Grilles are like teeth on a person. If the grille insert (ironically, also called grille teeth by many car enthusiasts) isn't straight and perfect, you hardly notice it, but if any part of the insert is bent, frayed, or scratched, the blemish grabs your attention right away, much like a piece of spinach trapped between somebody's teeth.

Ditto for a hood ornament or radiator cap, only they're like a person's nose. If the schnoz doesn't visually go with the face, it looks terribly out of place.

Grille inserts on a roadster can also help define the car. Painted-on numbers to mimic an old race car, vintage badges affixed to the grille teeth or positioned in front to emphasize the old car's heritage, or even a custom grille insert can help set the tone for a car's styling theme. This chapter brushes up on some interesting grille teeth and radiator caps that you might see at a rod run or cruise night.

2   Scott DePron built his 1932 Ford roadster to emulate the racers of the historic Mines Field Races that took place from 1932 to 1936 in Los Angeles. The old badges lend to the intended effect.

3   Sometimes the simplest statements are the most profound. Lewis Wolff's 1932 Ford coupe retains all the original goods; only the club plaque is non-stock.

4   Rodders during the early era—the 1930s through the 1940s in particular—often placed the front license plate wherever it was handy, even on the light crossbar.

5   I think this radiator cap says it all. The connection to water (in this case, hot water) is obvious, and despite the spigot's everyday household use, it looks so appropriate here.

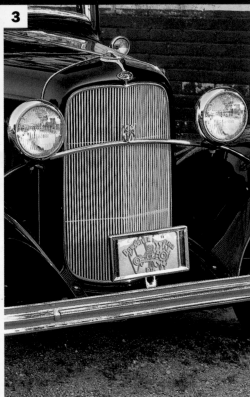

6

6 Tom Leonardo crafted this radiator cap for his 1930 Ford roadster. The centerpiece spins from the wind pushing the small half cups on the axis.

7 The theme here is racing, and Howard Holman uses the number 27 to stick to that topic. It also denotes the year of his modified Ford roadster.

8 A pair of 1933 Pontiac grilles were joined together to form the unique radiator housing for Ed Iskenderian's legendary 1924 Ford.

9 There's plenty to look at on Iskenderian's roadster. He had the radiator ornament custom made, and it even includes his name as part of the emblem.

7

8

9

10   Iskenderian cast this winged radiator cap while he was in his high school shop class. Notice that today he has it wired to the radiator to prevent theft.

11   Another member from the old guard, Gabby Garrison mounted this winged skull on his 1925 Ford. He was a hot rodder in the 1930s, and he built this car when he was over 80 years old.

12   This photo shows the cleverness behind Jake Jacobs' hand-painted Ford tub. You can see the decoupage on the hood and the patina on the radiator cap, and note the hand-painted fly.

13 Track-T roadsters are among my favorite hot rods because they bring another element of the racetrack to the street. If chrome plating is too expensive, you can cover the insert with paint.

14 This front shot of Dennis Love's 1927 Ford illustrates the simplistic beauty that can be found in a traditional hot rod. This picture makes me want to jump in the car and drive it like I stole it.

15 After giving the hood on his 1958 Chevy a quick shave, Danny Osburn finished the job with quality chrome plating, a top-class paint job, and some welcome pinstripes.

16 The golden era for car design must have been the 1930s. Designers were learning about streamlining, and they gave cars their individual touches, like this greyhound dog on a 1936 Ford radiator.

17 The cloud-filled blue sky of Utah's Great Basin reflects off the chrome on this 1934 Ford's radiator shell trim. The red pinstripes are a fitting accent to this piece.

18 Oh, how the auto designers of the 1950s understood the wonders of chrome! By lowering this 1956 Olds, the car takes on a serious demeanor.

19 Trim the emblems off the hood, remove the vertical bumper guards, and give the grille a custom insert, and you have a typical street custom car.

20 The 1955 DeSoto grille teeth have been used on countless other cars for a custom look. Here's an unusual treatment—they're on Glenn Matejel's 1955 DeSoto!

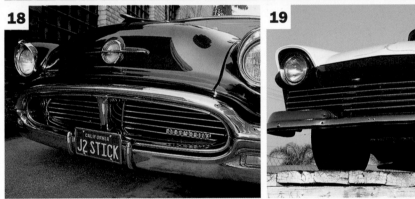

1 The timid lines of a Ford Model A can become aggressive simply by chopping the top a few inches. This car's straight window posts make this task a little easier than most other chop jobs.

2 Convert that old family sedan into a hot rod by dropping the fenders and chopping the top. This 1932 Ford Tudor has a few inches removed from its top.

Body Treatments:
Chopped Tops

As with many hot rod concepts and styling ideas, the treatment of chopping a car's top was conceived on the dry lakebeds of Southern California. And, as with many of those ideas, the concept behind chopping a top was to reduce the car's front area for better top speed (no pun intended).

Chopping a car's top isn't an easy task, though, and requires skillful planning and execution. Get it wrong, and that roof is going to fit like a mixed-up jigsaw puzzle. But done right, the car will look sleek and smooth—just the way the dry lakes racers intended it back in the day.

3 One of the most familiar chop jobs is the *American Graffiti* coupe, which started life as an ordinary 1932 Ford five-window.

4 Chopped convertible tops are often referred to as Carson tops, a name derived from the shop in Carson, California, where many of the custom car builders went for their tops back in the late 1940s and early 1950s.

5 George DuVall is considered the father of the split windshield for hot rod roadsters. Later, Doane Spencer used one of the famous "V" windshields on his roadster, shown here.

6 The classy lines of a 1933–1934 Ford three-window coupe aren't lost when its top is chopped. In fact, some rodders say that the shortened roof actually makes the car look better.

7 In an effort to reduce frontal area, dry lakes racers used to chop the windshields on their roadsters. They'd also position the flat chunk of glass slightly rearward for better aerodynamics.

8 Just to remind you what a non-chop job is, here's Dave Crouse in his rather original 1932 Ford five-window.

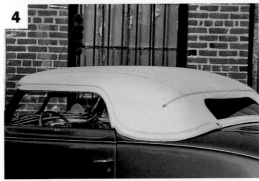

LOUVERS

Louvers are for lovers. Okay, that's being a little extreme, but those slivered sections of sheet metal can certainly lend a romantic look to any hot rod. Louvers were originally intended to help aerate engine compartments, relieving them of heat buildup from the engine. In some situations, they even helped minimize uplift for a car's rear section at speed when making a high-speed pass over the Southern California dry lakebeds.

Louvers continue to be used to ventilate engine compartments, but their primary use today is for styling purposes. The notches are cut in the sheet metal with steel-hardened dies that actually tear and form the metal. By spacing the dies over a pattern, a good louver-layer (if I may use that term) can create a design that's unique and particular to the intended hot rod. Here are some of my favorite louver patterns that I've photographed.

The side louvers are what Henry Ford's crew originally placed on this 1934 Ford's hood. The four rows on the hood's top were added years later.

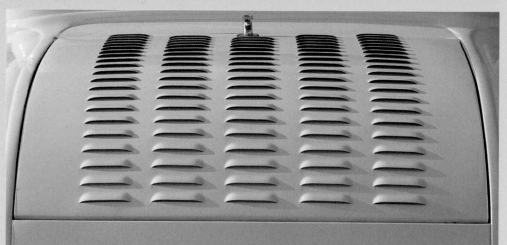

Five rows of about 20 louvers distinguish the lid for this car's rumble seat. Notice that the center row is slightly off center, obviously a mistake by the louver-layer.

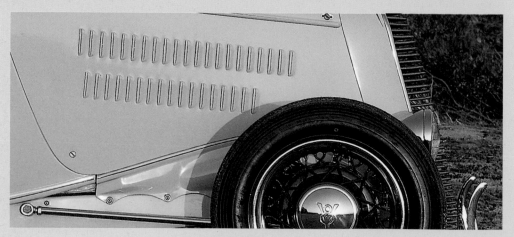

Jake Jacobs crafted the side panels for his 1934 Ford's hood and then laid out two rows of louvers to help keep his hot rod engine cool.

One way to make the aluminum side blister—created to clear the Hemi engine's valve cover—is to make it look like it belongs. The louvered pattern around it was just the trick.

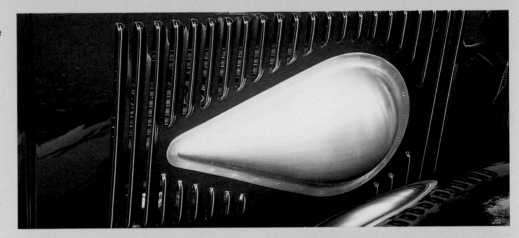

Louvers can serve as their own palette for painting, too. The dual pinstripes on each draw attention to the louvers without distracting the viewer's eye.

Taking care when laying out the louver pattern is important to ensure that everything is symmetrical. The pinstripes on the radiator shell help draw the eye toward the louvers.

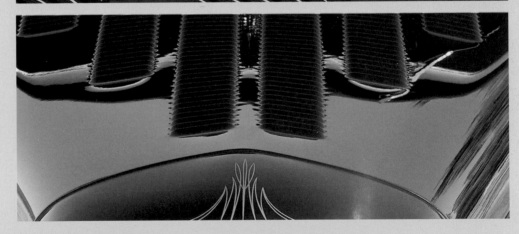

A picture is worth a thousand words, but in this case the louvers do some of the talking. Each louver contains the signature of a famous hot rodder. Recognize some of them?

Body Treatments:
Miscellaneous—It's Those Little Things That Sometimes Matter

As mentioned already, I subscribe to the rule that the first rule about hot rodding is that there are no rules. Due to that rule, and to those who also follow it, you see a lot of interesting detail work on the individual cars at rod runs and shows. This chapter salutes some of the detail work that might otherwise be overlooked. So, put away your magnifying glass for now because we've made the images large enough on these pages for you to see the little things that matter.

2　The small blister on the cowl makes room for the steering box on the Doane Spencer roadster.

3　When to shave, and when not to? This pickup truck still has its Custom Cab emblem.

4　Von Dutch decals always lend a rebellious twist to any hot rod.

5　John Athan set the rear windshield of a 1940 Chrysler as a front windshield on his 1929 Ford.

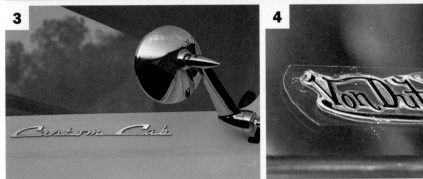

6

7

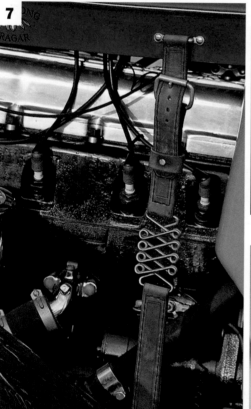

8

9

10

6   The wood braces on this Ford phaeton add a level of refinement to the car.

7   The leather hood straps are reason enough not to have side aprons on this Model A.

8   Nose art similar to that on World War II bombers is a nice touch. This is on a 1932 Ford—you know, a Deuce.

9   Event decals are a good way to help chronicle your hot rod's history.

10   Whose car is this, anyway? It probably belongs to a guy named Armstrong who has a Cragar four engine in it.

11 Spotlights on a 1950s custom are always nice additions.

12 Sometimes even a simple cotter key put in the right place can make a hot rod look so refined.

13 Speed plaques placed on the car's dashboard lend a timeless look to any hot rod.

14 I took this picture of Hank Becker while riding in his 1926 Model T hot rod. I really enjoy the composition, with his old aviator's hat against a backdrop of a modern building and car.

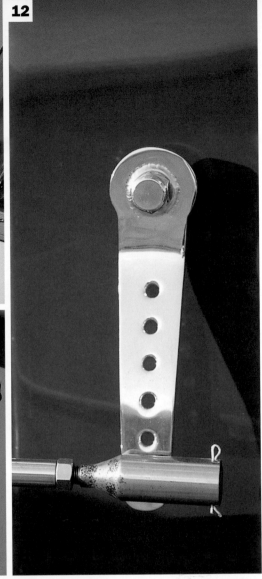

15

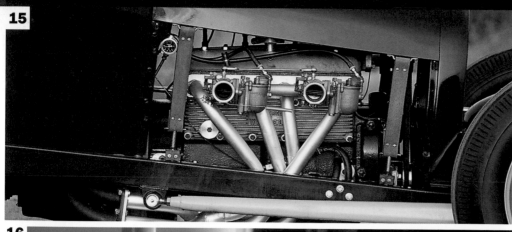

16

17

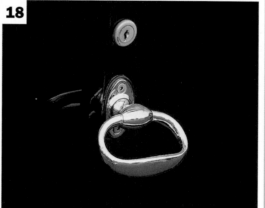

18

19

15   There are those cool leather hood straps again! Check out the gauge in front of the firewall.

16   The 90 MPH Club was a real deal back in the day. This is an original plaque.

17   This tire cover was hand-painted back in the 1930s. Fortunately, it has survived the years.

18   John Buttera was a genius. Even though his 1926 Ford sedan was the forerunner of today's modern hot rod, he chose an original Model T door handle for his car.

19   An aftermarket headlamp housing with flames is a nice alternative to original parts.

20   That Von Dutch guy—what a character!

21   In case you never tire of pinstripes and decals, there's always the firewall.

22   That original Bonneville/ *Hop Up* magazine 1951 decal is too good to remove.

23   This NSRA nationals award plaque was placed by its owner on the car's steering column drop.

24   In addition to his timing tag chronicling his 120-mile-per-hour top speed at El Mirage in 1942, Ed Iskenderian displays one of his company's own speed tags.

25   As the timing tag indicates, Doane Spencer painted the number 389 on his car for a pass over El Mirage Dry Lake in 1950. The car reached a speed of 126.76 miles per hour.

20

21

22

23

24

25

Interiors:
Upholstery, Carpet, and Trunks

In terms of real time spent with a car, most of it brings you in contact with the car's interior. Oh, we poke and prod a lot under the hood, and we've been known to crawl on our backs like infantrymen under fire as we snoop beneath the car to chase a mechanical gremlin. For the most part, though, when we plant our fannies on the driver's or passenger's seat, we're there for the duration of the ride.

And so it should be, too, that you spend a lot of time deciding just what kind of interior you're going to give your hot rod. At the end of the day, if you're not happy with the experience, you'll be less prone to jump in the car again for a relaxing drive across town or across country.

Here are a few interiors ideas that might just make you feel at home.

2 Shown here is classic tuck-and-roll (also known as rolled-and-pleated) upholstery, which never goes out of style.

3 The fabric seats on this Model A offer a cooler, more comfortable experience than Naugahyde, vinyl, or even leather.

4 The carpet inserts are made of the same material as the interior's permanent carpet. One saves the other from excessive wear.

5 The rolled-and-pleated pattern on this car is wider than you'll see on many hot rod seats and door panels.

6 If you're into rat rods, then live it up. Don't worry so much about the finished product but, rather, how you treat today!

7

8

9

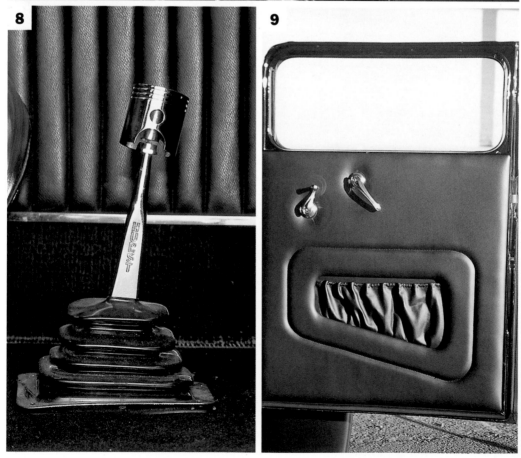

7 Want to protect your car's upholstery? Nothing more than a section from an old rug will sometimes do the trick.

8 This is the Hurst floor shifter on the *American Graffiti* coupe. You can see that the carpet is worn and frayed.

9 Storage space is limited in most hot rods, so a side pouch in the door panel is a welcome addition.

10 Diamond-tuft or square-tuft upholstery always adds a bit of elegance. This is the crew quarters of a 1958 Cadillac.

11 Everybody pays attention to the wood sides of a woodie, but if you look inside and then up, you'll see some interesting woodwork.

12 This 1938 Chevrolet was treated to new upholstery, which was laid out to emulate what was originally supplied with the car.

13 Here's a timeless look. Jim DeLorenzo finished the interior to his 1940 Ford Deluxe coupe in the early 1960s. When I photographed it in 1990, it still looked brand new.

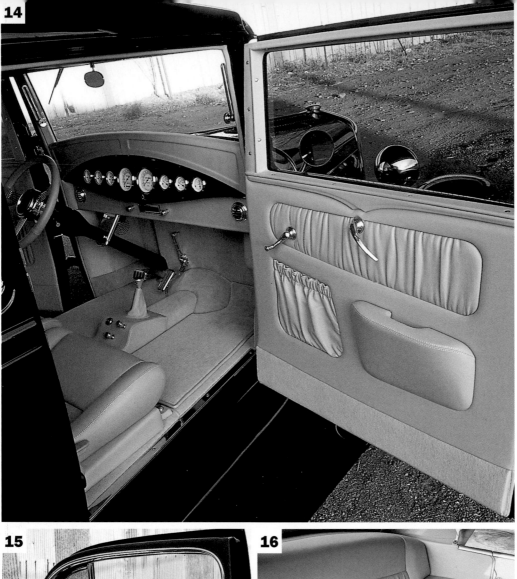

14 The panel inserts on the door give this all-leather interior an even richer look.

15 White door panels do wonders for brightening up an interior. The reflective light makes the car's interior look larger and more inviting.

16 Don't forget the back seat. Arm rests, seat belts, and generously padded seats give a welcoming appearance.

17 Finishing the trunk with upholstery that matches the interior can give your hot rod a show-quality appearance.

18   This roadster's gas tank is concealed within the carpeted bulkhead inside the trunk.

19   This old Ford's trunk has been modernized with tuck-and-roll upholstery and a stainless-steel prop.

20   Choices of fabric, carpeting, and even design patterns can play significant roles in how an interior will look.

21   A set of hidden stainless-steel hinges and the aluminum hydraulic damper make this deck lid easy to open and close.

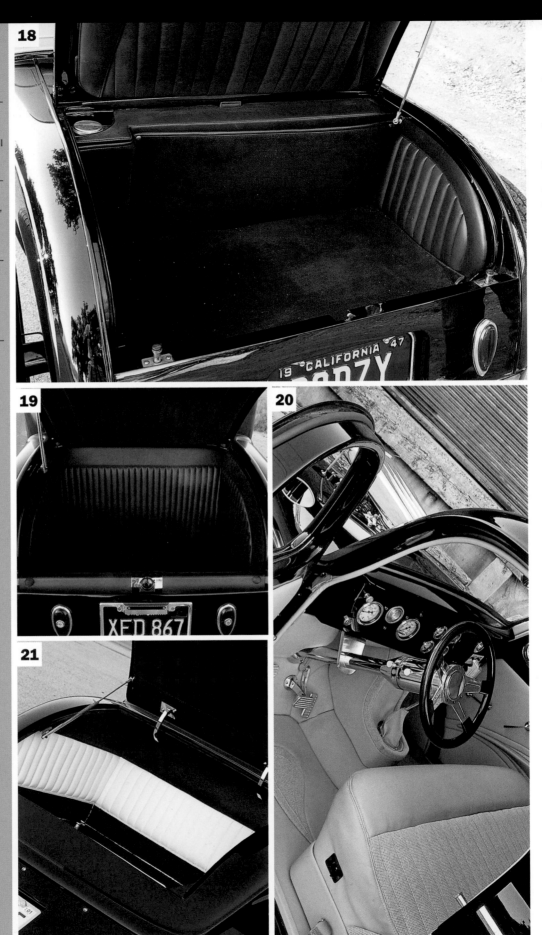

22

23

24

25

22 Spartan interiors sometimes lend a casual feel to a hot rod. This dash is stock, and the shift knob an aftermarket add-on.

23 This all-white interior jumps to life thanks to a little chrome on the window garnish moldings and the red dashboard.

24 A few subtle details, such as the maroon piping on the upholstery and the cut-down steering wheel, set this interior apart from others.

25 Careful measuring and shopping can help you select a set of bucket seats that will fit an early Ford like this one.

26 This 1957 Ford's dashboard is dressed with custom knobs and bright red paint.

27 The back seat has been upholstered to simulate the front bucket seats on this Ford Victoria.

28 The door panels and seats on this 1956 Ford have been stitched to resemble the original factory patterns.

29

30

31

32

29 One of the nice things about a 1950s dashboard is the acres and acres of chromed trim.

30 Placement of the steering column and wheel is important for the driver's comfort.

31 The smoothed and filled dash gives this 1936 Ford a modern look. The steering column drop is styled to match.

32 Sometimes a pair of fuzzy dice hanging from the rearview mirror is all you need to create a custom car's interior.

33 Too much purple on this dashboard would have put it over the edge. The black top serves as a good accent.

34 Where to put the stereo? For years, hot rodders have been concealing it in the glove box.

35 Careful where you put those muddy feet! Fortunately, this rodder equipped his all-white carpet with matching inserts.

36 Gray tweed upholstery like this was especially popular during the late 1980s. It offers a cool feel during hot weather.

1 The openness of a roadster makes you feel as though you could just drop right in. Like the old rental car television commercial stated, "Let Hertz put you in the driver's seat."

2 There's something exciting about tucking behind a roadster's windshield. This shot gives you an idea what it's like.

Interiors:
Roadster Seats

When you think about it, there isn't much privacy in a roadster or phaeton hot rod. With the top down, driver and passenger are clearly visible, and when the car is parked, any bystander can view practically the whole interior.

Given that, it's rather important that you select the right style of seat and the proper upholstery for your hot rod roadster. There are countless options.

Here are a few.

3   This is the view that Ed Iskenderian sees every time he slips behind this big steering wheel.

4   Who said roadsters and convertibles have to be two-seaters? For years, rumble seats have served extra passengers.

5   Earth-tone colors have always been popular with roadster owners. Black on the steering wheel and shift boot cover provides good contrast.

6 Time hasn't been kind to this roadster's interior, but when coupled with the paint's patina, it all seems to come together.

7 The draft beer handle used for the shift knob makes a rebellious statement in this Deuce roadster's interior.

8 Black and red aren't the only colors hot rodders understand how to use. Check out these bright tones.

9 A little wood on the dash, an old Grant steering wheel, and an eight-ball shift knob give this roadster a high school hot rod theme.

10 Because sun and rain can be brutal, some rodders use marine-quality vinyl to upholster their open-top cars.

11 A few gauges never hurt. Obviously this driver likes to remain informed about his engine's vitals.

12 The engine-turned dash insert reflects this roadster's racing heritage. This was especially popular in the 1940s.

13 This Model A's interior is a mixture of old and new; the steering wheel and gauges to the left of it aren't stock.

14 This Model A's stock instrument cluster is complemented by two more gauges at the bottom.

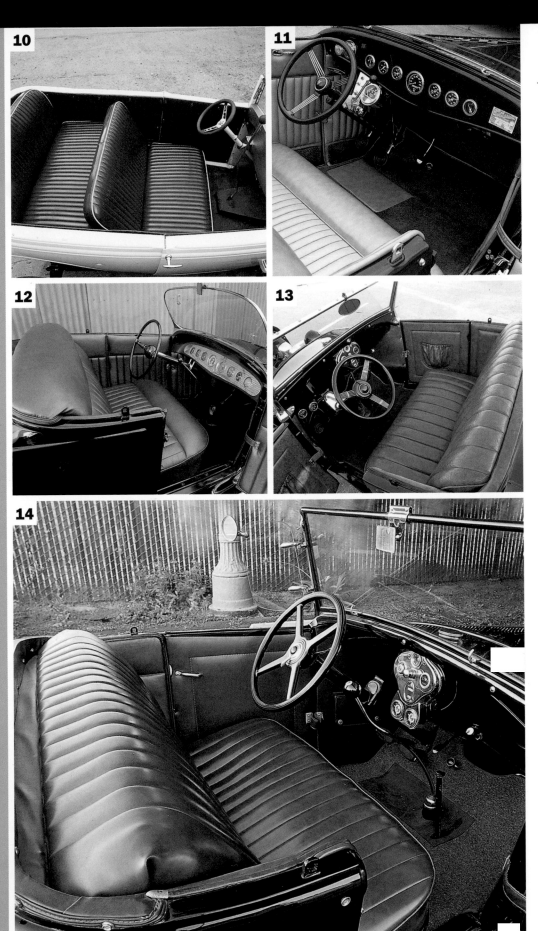

15 The wood floor and bare-bones controls in this modified roadster are similar to what you'd find in an old dry lakes racer.

16 Simple in design, yet plush in assembly, the interior to Mark Morton's 1929 Ford borders on elegance.

17 Believe it or not, this interior was assembled using old components lying around the garage.

18 Crushed velour, as seen in this Dan Woods–built T-bucket, was common among hot rods built in the 1970s.

19   Surplus bomber seats were favored by dry lakes racers after World War II, and the ones in this car are good examples of what they looked like.

20   The snap buttons on the body trim for this track-T hint that this car could be a racer.

21   The white pinstripes around the center-mount tachometer on this 1932 complement the car's white upholstery.

22   The steering column and engine-turned dash insert are fitting tributes to the late Doane Spencer in his restored Deuce roadster, now owned by Bruce Meyer.

Interiors:
Steering Wheels

The phrase "hands on" has real meaning when it comes to hot rodders and their steering wheels. No other part of the car becomes more intimate with drivers, because from the moment they steer their cars onto the street until they park at the local cruise spot, their hands are on the steering wheel—or at least they're supposed to be.

A stylish steering wheel is important, but perhaps of more relevance to the owner is the hoop's comfort when the owner grips it. If you're going to spend any amount of time behind your hot rod's steering wheel, then find one that's going to reward you with comfort as well as style. Hopefully some of the steering wheels featured here will help steer you in that direction.

2 Another Deuce Ford with a 1950s vintage Ford steering wheel belongs to Wayne Cash. Larger steering wheels also offer more leverage when making those tight turns in parking lots.

3 A popular steering wheel for Ford roadsters was the four-spoke wheel. This steering wheel is often referred to as the roadster wheel because it was originally developed for the roadster race cars that competed at Indianapolis and oval dirt tracks.

4 Replacing original-equipment steering wheels with modern hoops was a common practice among rodders back in the 1960s. Lewis Wolff planted this late-model Ford wheel on his Deuce coupe during that decade.

5 Column shifters aren't common on hot rods, so Hoke Hokinson left the shifter on the tree for his 1935 Ford pickup truck.

6 The setting sun casts a warm golden glow on the steering wheel that Dave Mathis pirated from a 1959 Chevrolet Impala for his 1934 Ford roadster.

7 This banjo steering wheel still sports its center-button horn and looks very cool in Martin Williams' 1936 Ford pickup.

8 If you remember the 1960s (though not too many people do!), then you'll probably recall the Grant three-spoke steering wheels that could be found in practically every speed shop in America. This silver metalflake wheel gives a hip look to Gary Moline's 1959 Ford F-100's interior.

9 Another variation of the old Grant steering wheel theme, this one with its spokes drilled, is seen in Morgwn Pennypacker's rat-rod roadster.

10 Lecarra makes several vintage-style steering wheels. This model resembles steering wheels that Detroit produced back in the 1950s.

Interiors:
Instruments and Gauges

I love looking at dashboards and instrument clusters on hot rods because they tell a lot about the car. You can gain a bit of automotive history just by looking closely at some of the vintage gauges that hot rodders have selected for their cars. I particularly enjoy the dashboards of 1950s American cars because they present a huge expanse of metal and chrome that we'll probably never see again from auto manufacturers anywhere in the world.

But even the simplest of dashes and instruments—a vintage Model A comes to mind—can look good when it's decorated with hot rod gauges. Something as simple as a steering-column tachometer or a set of gauges beneath the dashboard is enough to tell the world that this car is not your typical antique car.

As you can imagine, hot rodders have always come up with unique and interesting ways to set their dashboards and instrument clusters apart from those of other cars. You might say that a person can gauge the quality of your hot rod by its instruments.

2 The *American Graffiti* coupe sports a variety of gauge makes on its instrument cluster. The trio on the right is original Stewart Warner brand.

3 Want a modern look? Dakota Digital offers a wide variety of digital gauges, instruments, and dash inserts. While clearly not in the spirit of traditional hot rod styling, they provide a distinct look to the interior.

4 This cluster of Stewart Warner gauges in this 1932 Ford insert looks so right. There's a simplistic, yet elegant, look about them.

5 This Auburn-style dash and gauge insert gives this Model A roadster a smart look. The leather-stitched banjo steering wheel is a nice touch.

6 The late Tom McMullen designed this dash during the early 1960s for his 1932 Ford roadster. I especially like the pinstripes, which give added dimension to the gauges.

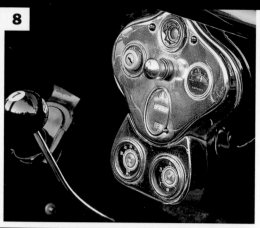

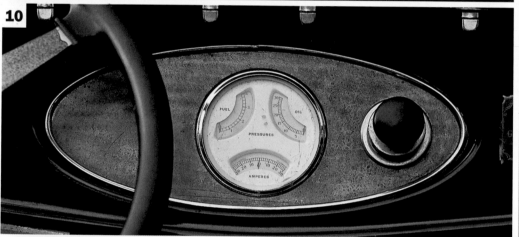

7 This Auburn dash, mounted in a 1929 Ford, includes Stewart Warner gauges and is complemented by a four-spoke roadster steering wheel.

8 Two gauges—in this case for water temperature and oil pressure—are carried in the custom add-on that mounts beneath the original Model A insert.

9 A good source for dash inserts can be found in the marine market. In this case, Chris Fuller put a speedboat dash insert in his 1927 Ford Model T.

10 Who says an instrument cluster has to look cluttered? Shop around and you can find a multitask gauge that looks vintage yet takes up little space on the dashboard.

11 By carefully selecting your instruments, you can give a modern billet dash a timeless look. These gauges are by Classic Industries.

12   A 1940 Ford dashboard always looks great, whether it's in near-stock form or dressed with this custom instrument cluster.

13   Some people—especially from the custom-car crowd—will tell you that you can never have too much chrome. Otherwise, this 1938 Ford's dash is pretty much stock.

14   Retaining the original gauges can still look sporty, especially if you surround them with custom add-ons like the dice knob handles and bolt-on oil pressure gauge beneath the dash.

15   Let's take that stock instrument theme one step further and include all cars. Original gauges in a 1950s-era car, such as this 1957 Oldsmobile's speedometer, can be particularly attractive.

16   Aftermarket auxiliary instruments are a quick way to give your hot rod its own look. Most gauge clusters bolt to the bottom of the dashboard.

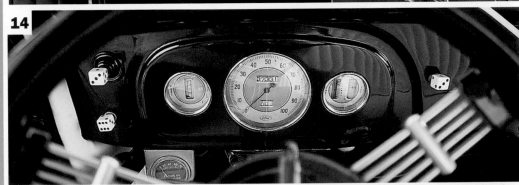

CHEAP TRICKS

It's time for a reality check, so let's put away the checkbooks for a moment and ask ourselves: Do we really need to spend a king's ransom to make our hot rods look cool? Some people say no, and for them it's just as honorable to shop for parts from a J. C. Whitney catalog or at the local flea market as it is to buy from some of the top aftermarket suppliers in the country. A little ingenuity and a humble heart are sometimes all that you'll need to complete the mission, too. Here, then, are some cheap tricks that I've seen hot rodders use.

The finishing touch to Dave Lukkari's dashboard includes a passel of autographs by some rather famous hot rod luminaries.

There's not a new part to be seen on the dash of Jake Jacobs' Model A, but you have to admit, it still looks cool.

Joe Haska spent less than $50 for the seat covers to his 1946 Ford Tudor. "They still held my big butt," he jokingly said.

A fresh coat of paint on the dash, a few vintage parts, and select use of some classic decals are enough to give Joshua Shaw's interior the "ride" stuff.

Upholstery? We don't need no stinkin' upholstery! Instead, a serape from nearby Tijuana, Mexico, will do just fine for Jonny Guilmet's 1956 Oldsmobile.

Gone are the door panels to Morgwn Pennypacker's 1951 Ford. The exposed bulkheads make a nice place to stash a spare bottle of engine oil and yesterday's coffee.

Sometimes keeping the original upholstery works best. Manny Betes had this blood-red Naugahyde put on his Model A's seat back in 1940.

This is about as basic as you can get. Doug Bobbie's 1932 Ford wasn't finished in time for the 50th anniversary of the Bonneville Nationals in 1998, so he plopped a seat on the frame rails, then headed for Wendover, Utah.

Here's another serape on a stock seat, this time in Rob Crouse's 1932 Ford highboy. Check out the goggles and aviator cap.

Steve Wickert bolted in a seat and quick-release seat belt to his Model A, then headed to the annual Antique Drags sponsored by the Forever Fours Car Club.

Drivetrains:
Engines

Face it, the heart of a hot rod is its engine. Even the name "hot rod" suggests that it's about the engine first; everything else is just secondary in importance.

So, in our quest for hot rod ideas, it's time for us to go to the heart of the matter and check out some hot rod engines. Most of this chapter is devoted to the engines themselves, but we'll take a look at some of the periphery engine components as well during our walk around.

When you review the following engines, keep in mind that we also owe a debt of gratitude to dinosaurs that lived and died long, long ago. It was those giant lizard-like creatures that gave their lives back then, so that today we can have fossil fuels to burn in our hot rod engines. Here's to you, Mr. T-Rex.

2 Rail dragsters evolved from hot rods. This one is powered by an inline four-cylinder engine.

3 Scroll engraving was popular back in the 1970s and could be found on various parts of the engine, including the carburetor's intake scoop.

4 This 390-cubic-inch Ford engine can be considered one of the first muscle engines. It's fed by two four-barrel carburetors.

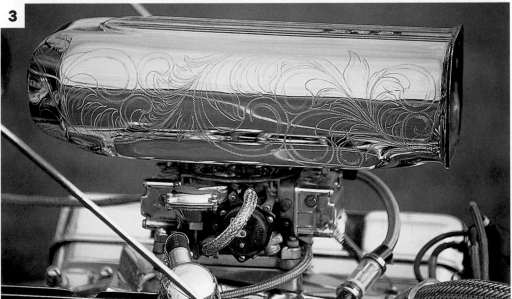

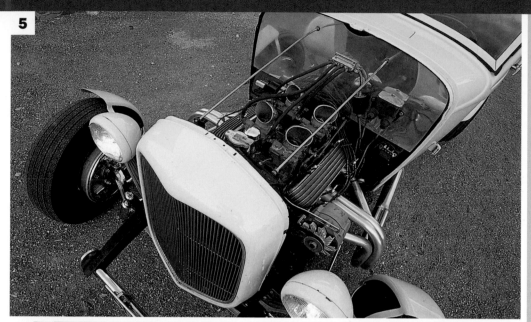

5 Even though some rodders consider small-block Chevy V-8s to be a dime a dozen, you can make yours unique by using some rare components. The *American Graffiti* coupe's 327 has a Man-A-Fre four-carb intake manifold, something you don't see very often.

6 The cylinder heads on Ed Iskenderian's Ford V-8 flathead were originally intended for trucks. The Maxi heads' valve covers are inscribed with Isky's name, something he did back in 1940.

7 Dick Williams originally built this flathead during the early 1950s, and the four-pot engine helped his car win the AMBR award in 1953.

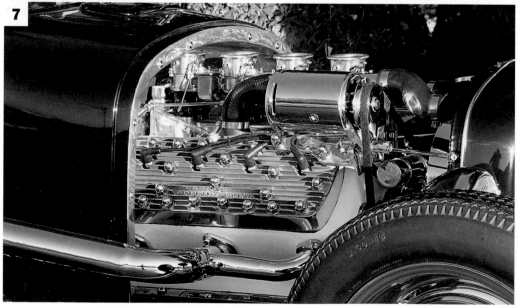

8 The engine bay on this 1956 Chevrolet is clean and tidy. It's nothing fancy, just a straightforward package that any rodder would be proud of.

9 Ever since Chrysler Corporation introduced the Hemi in 1953, this venerable V-8 has been favored by hot rodders, who have put this engine in all sorts of cars. Ironically, this DeSoto Firedome Hemi remains in its original 1955 package.

10 Even though this Cadillac engine displaces a whopping 512 cubic inches (thanks to 0.030-inch overbore pistons), there's plenty of space left in this 1953 Ford truck's engine bay to see the road underneath.

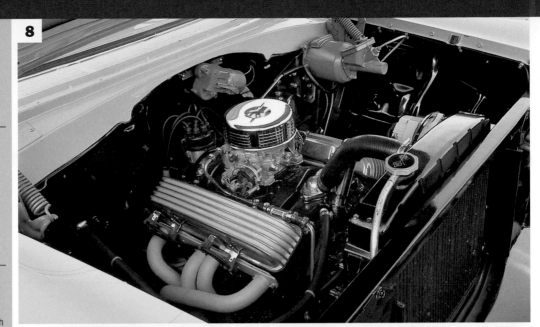

11

12

13

11   Here's another clean—and complete—engine bay from a 1950s-vintage hot rod. Chevrolet 350 V-8 engine swaps are especially popular for these cars.

12   Even though there's not much chrome, this Ford V-8 flathead catches the eye. The bright green paint helps make it pop.

13   Here's a classic 1950s look: brass radiator, copper fuel lines, and a painted firewall.

14 Contrasting colors, in this case blue and yellow, make this engine stand out even more against the bright red fenders.

15 Bernie Couch has owned his 1932 Ford roadster since 1940, and its most recent engine is this 1939 Mercury V-8 flathead that boasts a Potvin camshaft.

16 Ed Winfield was among the first to develop high-performance cylinder heads for early Ford fours. If you can find one today, buy it!

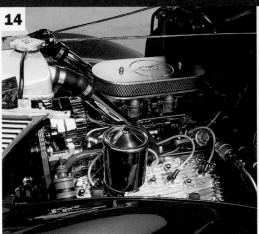

17 Here's another example of a Chevrolet small-block in an early Ford. The tri-power intake gives this combination a nasty look.

18 This rebuilt 1954 Chrysler Hemi has Parker valve covers, and the handmade exhaust headers are heat-treated.

19 There's probably not a better hot rod to use to show off an exhaust system than a T-bucket. The tiny roadster allows all sorts of variations.

20 Small-block Chevys have become the paramount engine of choice for hot rodders, but there's another small-block on the block that warrants attention. I'm talking about Ford's 260-289-305 family. Indeed, one of these small-blocks was the engine that Carroll Shelby planted in his first Cobra.

21 Another Ford favorite is this mucho-grande big-block that wears the famous Ford Racing logo on its valve covers.

22 Keep it simple, keep it clean. Although there's really not much to see under this hot rod's hood, the engine is clean and presentable.

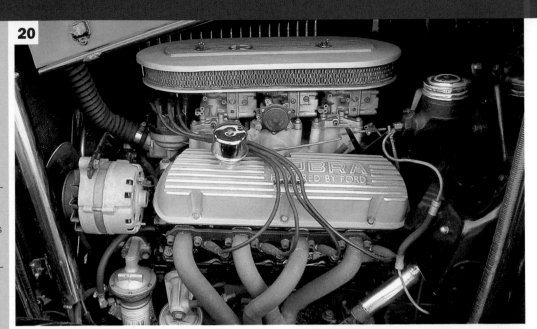

23 There's nothing fancy about this old Ford six-cylinder, but a few chromed acorn nuts on the cylinder head liven it up.

24 In 1937 Ford introduced its V-8 60, a small-displacement engine, to replace the aged four-cylinder as the company's baseline engine. The 60 stands for the engine's power, 60 horsepower. Many of the companies that offered speed equipment for the full-size V-8 also made performance parts for the V-8 60.

25 This 1950 Ford V-8 flathead displaces 260 cubic inches, runs a Potvin three-quarter race cam, carries two Stromberg 97 carbs on its Offenhauser manifold, and relies on Speedway's center-dump manifolds to expel the exhaust.

26 You can dare to be different and place a Model A, B, or C Ford four-cylinder in your hot rod. This Model C has a 1/8-inch overbore for 214 cubic inches. It has a Riley four-port head (two intake valves per cylinder) that is fed by a pair of Weber 45 DCOE side-draft carburetors.

27 Built in the spirit of the old days, this car's V-8 flathead sports straight-through exhausts and a high-rise intake manifold.

28 Another Ford four uses a 216-cubic-inch Model B with a Cragar cylinder fed by a pair of Stromberg 97 carburetors.

29

30

31

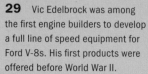

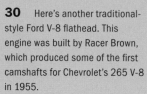

29 Vic Edelbrock was among the first engine builders to develop a full line of speed equipment for Ford V-8s. His first products were offered before World War II.

30 Here's another traditional-style Ford V-8 flathead. This engine was built by Racer Brown, which produced some of the first camshafts for Chevrolet's 265 V-8 in 1955.

31 Minimal chrome and bright colors earmark this Ford V-8 flathead.

32 I like the mechanical linkage that's used to modulate the carburetors on this Ford four with a Cragar cylinder head.

33 There's something visceral about Scott DaPron's Winfield-equipped Ford four that kept my attention longer than normal when I photographed it in 1997. The Winfield SRDD carbs and Cragar exhausts were especially compelling for me.

34 This Model A sports the vaunted Winfield Red Head. Ed Winfield was considered one of the top engine builders and tuners before World War II.

35 Another speed specialist from the prewar era was George Riley. He built various cylinder heads for the Ford four, including this four-port design. Another landmark brand was Mallory, maker of this engine's ignition.

36 A white firewall with pinstripes and a remote beehive oil filter give this 1932 Ford a look that was common back in the 1950s. The DeSoto Firedome Hemi engine adds to the look of the period.

1 A pair of Winfield carburetors found a home on this Model B Ford four-cylinder engine.

Drivetrains:
Multiple Carburetors

You can never have too many carburetors on a hot rod engine. Nope, in fact, the more the merrier, and for years hot rodders have lived by that adage.

Two- and three-carb setups are probably the most popular. For years, two- and three-pot manifolds were the trend among hot rodders with Ford V-8 flatheads.

When the overhead valve (OHV) V-8 became the engine of choice, single- and dual-quad manifolds became vogue, as were the tri-power OHV engines, using a trio of two-barrel carbs.

So, let's get going and see what's available in the world of multiple carburetors. It's time to carb up!

2 You don't need chrome to make carburetors look right on an engine. I like these gray two-barrels.

3 Some of the most stylish intake manifolds were created during the early days of hot rodding when the industry was rife with Ford V-8 flathead speed equipment.

4 This old flathead carries two Stromberg 97s on its manifold. These carbs have been popular ever since the 1930s when they were first introduced. The 97 stands for the venturi size in one-hundredths of an inch.

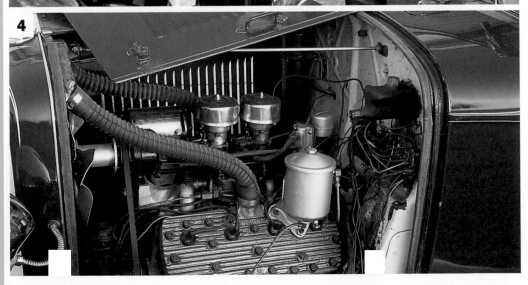

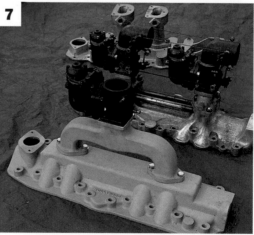

5 There's nothing better than a six-pack to go. And for good measure, George Krikorian had his half-dozen Stromberg 97s chrome plated.

6 Double trouble? Not really. Gary Moline put in a highly polished stainless-steel firewall to reflect the two four-barrel carbs on his Buick nailhead engine.

7 Looking for some cheap entertainment? Hustle on down to the local auto swap meet and check out the goods. I snapped this photo at an L.A. Roadster Show swap meet.

8 As the sign says, this is a rare Sharp intake manifold for a Ford V-8 flathead. The owner was asking $200 in the year 2000. No telling what it's worth today.

9 The mix of rare and machined aluminum works well to set this engine apart from others. I especially like the spun-aluminum venturi stacks.

10 Chevrolet offered tri-power on its 409 and 427 engines. Careful scrounging at the swap meets can net you a factory setup.

11 This three-pot Offenhauser manifold sports the old standby—Stromberg 97 carbs.

12 You can tell that this Model A is driven more than on occasional Sundays. Sometimes the gummy varnish on the carbs gives the car its own character.

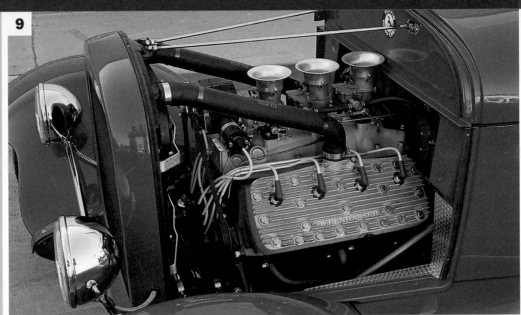

13

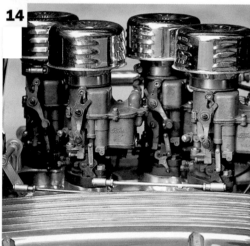

14

15

16

13   A combination of anodized, bead-blasted, and natural-finish parts gives this hot rod engine a rugged look.

14   You don't see many four-carb setups on OHV V-8s, which makes this engine unique in a sea of Chevrolet small-blocks fed by single four-barrel carbs.

15   Chevy stovebolt six-cylinder engines offer a nice change. This one, in a 1951 Chevrolet, has an Offenhauser manifold crowned with three one-barrel carbs.

16   Some people feel that the Weber side-draft carburetor is an exotic design, while others say the Italian carb offers an infinite range of tuning options.

17   A little bit of red paint, some polishing here and there, and some chrome linkage are enough to make this hot rod engine bridge the gap to the good ol' days.

18   Another good use of color combination is enough to make you look twice at this engine. The bell air cleaners give it an old-school look.

19   Tri-power on a Chevy small-block. This package is simple, rugged, and dependable—and oh, so cool.

20   This is one of the "oldest-school" engines I've photographed. It's the Model T engine with a rare Gemsa single OHV cylinder head that powers Hank Becker's 1926 Ford roadster.

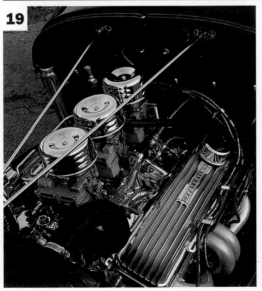

Drivetrains:
Supercharngers and
Fuel Injection

Looking for a quick answer to more horsepower? If so, then you might consider an old Bob Dylan tune that says the answer is "blowing in the wind"—in this case, by superchargers. When it comes to big horsepower, few things answer the call like a mighty supercharger—also called a blower—on a big-inch American V-8 engine. Top Fuel drag racers learned that long ago when they began strapping discarded 6-71 GMC blowers that were typically used for diesel trucks onto their race engines. Those big Roots-style blowers, affectionately called "Jimmies" by the racers, could stuff a lot of air and fuel into an engine, and as any engine builder will tell you, air and fuel are the primary ingredients for horsepower.

Hot rod engine builders found another way, in addition to big-lobe camshafts, high-compression pistons, and radical ignition timing, to gain more power. They learned that a good fuel injection system works wonders for squirting raw fuel precisely where it's needed on its way into the combustion chambers, since unlike carburetors, fuel injection can be governed better by the engine tuner.

But let's not kid ourselves. One of the most alluring aspects of superchargers and fuel injection on a hot rod engine is their visual appeal. So let's sneak a peek under some hoods and scoops to check out a few examples.

2   A classic blown hot rod engine can be found in the Tom McMullen roadster. The original car was built back in the early 1960s; this is a replica that *Street Rodder* magazine's staff assembled in 1998.

3   Those two four-barrel carburetors feeding the supercharger gather air through a scoop that was common on 1960s-era dragsters.

4

5

6

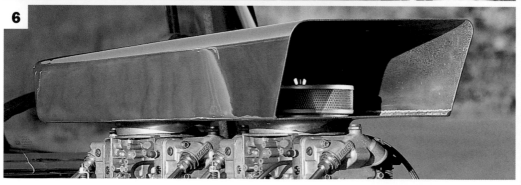

4 Like anything on a hot rod, even the supercharger can be personalized. The fuel lines leading up to the two Holley carburetors look like something you'd see at the drag strip.

5 One way to keep the gremlins out of the intake stacks when you're parked is to pack them with . . . gremlins.

6 I like this simple, yet functional, air scoop that also houses the carburetors' air filters.

7 One of the first hot rods to use fuel injection was built by Tommy Ivo back in the mid-1950s. His system was based on Hilborn's mechanical-drive fuel injection.

8 Notice how the four carburetors on this supercharged 327 Chevy V-8 are positioned just below the hood's line.

9 Don't want to rely on old-school technology for your hot rod's powertrain? Today's high-tech electronic fuel injection might be for you.

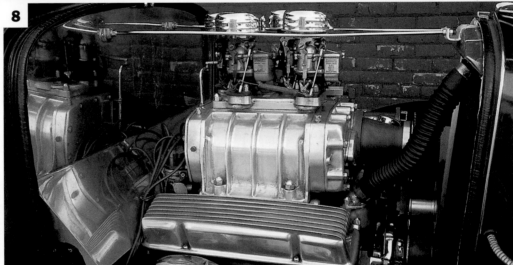

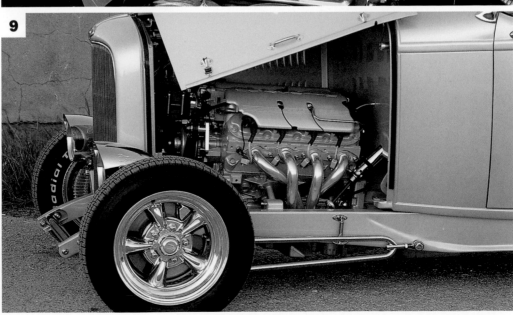

1 For years, chrome plating was the typical finish on a set of exhaust headers, but recently heat-treatment coatings have proven not only beneficial for promoting better exhaust flow, but they're also easy to maintain.

2 Be creative! The exhausts on the Doane Spencer car are routed through a portion of the classic Deuce frame rails and terminate just below the doors. When it came to style, Doane was one who never settled for the ordinary.

Drivetrains:
Exhausts

What goes in must come out, and that in a nutshell explains why we have exhaust systems in our cars. Hot rods are no different, but as you'll see, hot rodders have some ingenious and striking methods for making their exhaust systems visually appealing.

We could get into a long exposé about exhaust pipe design theory, but we won't. Instead, let's just direct our attention to some examples of hot rod exhaust designs. When you're finished, please head for the exit so we can proceed to the next chapter.

3   Here it is, a typical chrome-plated exhaust system on a T-bucket. It's not uncommon to see exhaust "bluing" at the junction of the pipes and exhaust ports. The culprit is excessive heat from the combustion chamber.

4   Sometimes, though, a simple set of dual exhaust pipes that dump the fumes and noise to the back of the car or truck will suffice. This is especially true for traditional rods that utilize an abundance of bolt-on parts.

5   This roadster's final drive includes a Halibrand quick-change center section, so the owner, Chris Fuller, kept the exhaust tips out of view. That way when you inspect the back section, you see the Halibrand first.

6 The tapered exhaust pipes on this 1932 Ford roadster are reminiscent of the exhaust systems found on the Indy track roadsters of the 1940s and 1950s. When the caps on the ends are "uncorked," you hear the exhaust's true sound!

7 Collector exhaust systems get their name because the individual exhaust header pipes collect into a single box. A collector box's primary benefit is the scavenging effect it has on the exiting exhaust gases.

8 If you count the exhaust headers on this engine, you will see three per side. In reality, though, that's a Ford V-8 flathead (with modified heads), and its two center exhaust ports siamese into a single hole to create this unique look.

9 Here's another exhaust cap that essentially closes a secondary exhaust system. Under normal conditions, the exhaust is routed through mufflers and tailpipes. For performance, and more noise, uncork the caps.

6

7

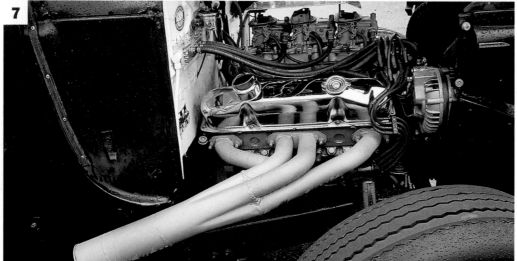

8

10 How tight can you make these exhaust headers? It takes a skilled pair of hands to route these large-diameter exhaust headers between the engine and frame rails before pointing them to the rear of the car.

11 This bug's-eye view of this truck's custom-made exhaust system reveals how clean a system can be. The entire system, from the header pipes and collector boxes to the exhaust tips, is made of stainless steel.

12 The mufflers are only slightly larger in diameter than the exhaust pipes that lead through them. Exhaust systems are generally fabricated after the car's suspension has been engineered and put in place.

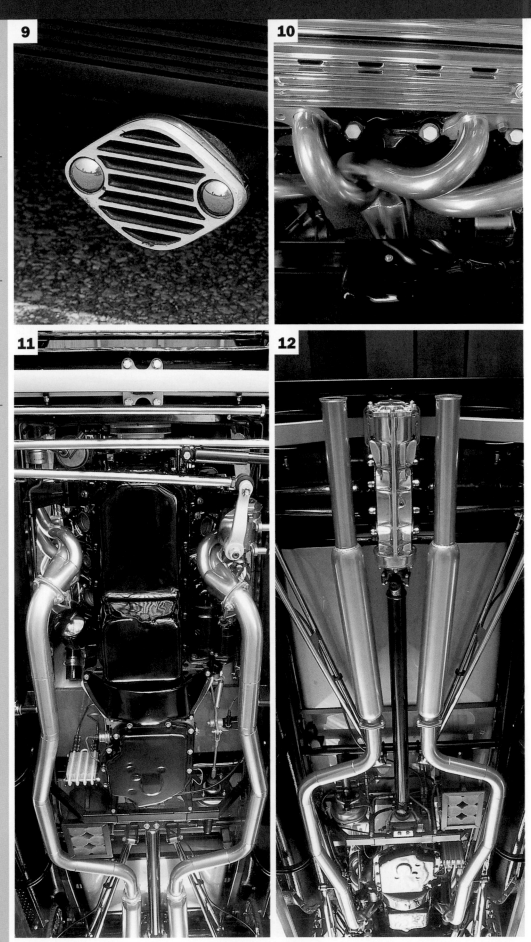

13 Typically, the tailpipes will be routed over the rear axle housings so they won't drag on the pavement or hit steep driveway reveals. The major factor to consider here, though, is the placement of the car body over the pipes.

14 How you terminate the exhaust system is up to you. The conventional style is to leave it as a single exit hole, but this hot rod will reveal two pairs of pipes to anybody following close behind.

15 Here's another example of an exhaust system that has been treated with aluminized coating, which can come in various styles and colors. This particular one has more of a natural metal finish to it.

16 Among the most striking pieces of a 1932 Ford are its frame rails, which become even more obvious when you build a highboy. Joe Nitti used his Deuce's frame rails to guide the exhaust pipes.

17 When it comes to exhaust headers for a Ford V-8 flathead, many rodders favor the name Fenton. Fenton headers were available as cast (here) or welded tubing.

18 Few engines command as much attention as a Chrysler Hemi. Keeping that in mind, Darryl Roberts kept the exhaust system for his 1932 Plymouth roadster as simple and straightforward as possible so the engine gets its due attention.

19 The exhaust on the famed Bill Neikamp 1929 Ford roadster terminates through the car's belly pan.

20 Don't forget the door-slammers! Although the hood and fenders conceal most of the car's exhaust, you can use a set of "lakes pipes" to join the show. The name "lakes pipes" originated at the dry lakes, where racers used designs similar to this.

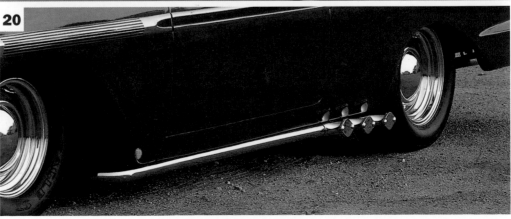

1 A good chassis begins with a solid frame, and the way to ensure you have that is by hiring a builder who knows what he or she is doing with a welder.

Drivetrains:
Chassis

Sometimes people confuse the terms *frame* and *chassis*, thinking that they're one and the same. They're not. In reality, a frame is one component of the chassis, which is also composed of the axles, brakes, and suspension components like the shocks and springs. In essence, the frame is what holds most of those components, making it perhaps the most integral part of the chassis.

Generally hot rods are built on existing frames, or on custom-made frames. Either way, the frame rails serve the same function of forming the backbone for the car. In addition to the chassis components, usually the frame supports the car's body and complete drivetrain. So let's give the frame its due, and do the same for the chassis.

2 Once the chassis is finished and the car's running, it's time to take it out and play with it! Going head to head against your buddy's hot rod can be fun, too.

3 If you're looking to keep your hot rod authentic, then you'll need a set of friction shock absorbers that Henry Ford's crews used back in the day.

4 This 1932 Ford roadster has all the classic trimmings. The body is rolled on the rear, and the chassis sports a transverse buggy spring over its quick-change rear end.

5 Jake Jacobs' 1934 Ford coupe boasts an army of louvers on the deck lid and roll pan, and the chassis rides on Model A springs hung from a Model A crossmember.

6

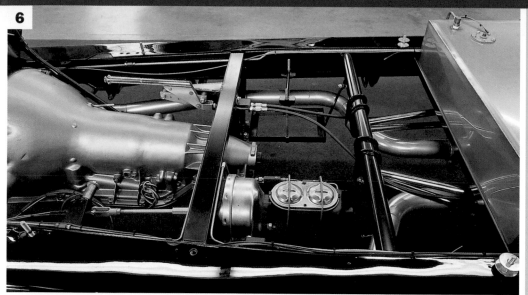

7

8

6   Crossmembers can be positioned practically anywhere a frame builder wants to put them. The left crossmember in this picture supports the transmission, while the right crossmember anchors this truck's rear suspension arms.

7   Jaguar's independent rear suspension was especially popular during the 1970s, and most of the systems were pirated from Jaguar's XKE model. One major advantage in terms of ride is the minimal unsprung weight from the system. The disc brakes are inboard, meaning they are mounted to the center section, so they contribute no additional weight to the rear suspension.

8   Many of the key elements to a complete chassis are still missing from this frame. The picture, however, does help illustrate the importance of a stout frame.

9 The front shock absorbers on this 1932 Ford roadster are anchored by a stanchion (on top of the shock) and the I-beam front axle.

10 No, this car isn't going so fast on the legendary Bonneville Salt Flats that its body blew off. Instead, Doug Bobbie hadn't finished the body, so he packed up his rolling chassis and headed to Utah for the 50th anniversary in 1998.

11 That's salt spray from a trip down the Bonneville Salt Flats on the frame rails and crossmembers of Doug Bobbie's car.

12 You can see the role that the rear crossmember plays in a chassis' design. It supports the rear spring, shock absorbers, nerf bars, and taillight.

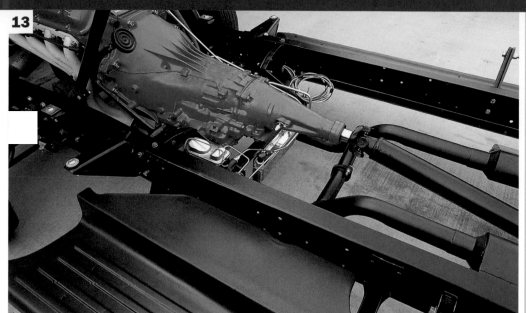

13

14

15

16

13 Most frame builders will box the frame rails to give them additional strength. This truck's frame rails have not been boxed.

14 You can almost hear the ready-to-roll 1932 Ford highboy roadster on the right say to the unfinished 1948 Ford truck beside it: "One day, you too will be a beautiful swan like me."

15 and 16 Same car, same frame, but two completely different views. One of the things I really enjoy about open-wheel hot rods is the view; you can see so much more of the car's chassis.

17 Traction bars are a common fix for a 1950s/1960s hot rod. As the name implies, the bars help locate the rear axle so that the drive tires can gain better traction during hard acceleration.

18 A rear end from a 1948 Ford was mounted using a Model A buggy spring to this hand-built frame. I like its simplicity.

19 and 20 Another good example of how much emphasis is placed, literally, on the frame.

21 John Buttera was one of the all-time great fabricators. His 1926 Ford Model T sedan is considered a milestone car, and his hand-built front suspension is one reason why.

22 The late John Buttera based his own independent rear suspension on a Jaguar third-member; the adjustable arms attach to its bottom.

23 This front view of Lil' John Buttera's Model T sedan helps illustrate just how sound, solid, and compact the car is.

24 Although the welds may look crude, they've held since 1932 when the Downey brothers built their Model T roadster. This is called a "suicide" front end, due to the placement of the axle. Sometimes the welds didn't hold, thus the suicide moniker.

25 Dick Williams constructed his frame from chrome-moly tubing, and to make it sit low he hung the front axle in a rather unique fashion. It, too, however, is considered a suicide front end.

26 This view of the front spring's center perch in relation to the axle helps illustrate why this is considered a suicide front end.

27 Dan Woods built a lot of T-buckets back in the 1970s, and this is one that has survived pretty much intact. Woods was especially known for using Jaguar independent rear suspension on his hand-built frames.

28 Here's another example of old-school technology looking cool. Notice how the brake line routes over and across the early Ford rear end.

29 Ford's 9-inch rear end—so named because its center section measures about 9 inches across—is one of hot rodding's favorites. This 1929 Ford uses a leaf spring for suspension on its boxed 1932 Ford frame.

1 There it is, an early "juice" brake. This 1940 Ford brake system is mounted to a 1929 Ford roadster, which originally used mechanical drum brakes.

Drivetrains:
Brakes

Okay, it's brake time, so let's forget about hot engines, solid frames, and smooth bodies. Instead, we're going to concentrate on ways to bring that hot rod to a halt.

Traditional hot rods look best with hydraulic brakes, or what the hot rod guys term "juice brakes," a phrase that was born out of Henry Ford's stubborn insistence that his cars come equipped with mechanical brakes as late as 1939. It wasn't until the fabled 1940 Ford that cars originating in Dearborn, Michigan, came equipped from the factory with hydraulic brakes. A common practice for dry lakes racers back in the late 1940s was to swap their cars' mechanical drum brake systems for 1940-and-later hydraulic systems. This was because the "juice" brakes work so

much better, thanks to brake fluid assuming most of the work load by forcing the brake shoes to expand and clamp down on their drums.

Most recently disc brakes have gained acceptance by rodders because the use of rotors and calipers presents an even greater leap forward in terms of stopping a car. Even so, traditionalists who favor the look of those old drum brakes have found ways to preserve some of that heritage, and we have cosmetic kits that give a disc brake the appearance of a drum.

But wait a minute, this is brake time, so let's cut to the chase and stop with the words so we can commence with the pictures. Here, then, are some cool hot rod brakes for your perusal.

2 Buick finned drum brakes from the late 1950s have always been popular. The fins help cool the brakes, as does the scoop that's been built into this system's backing plate.

3 Here's another shining example of an early Ford juice brake system. The hydraulic brake line feeds into the top of the backing plate, which holds the brake cylinder.

4 This rat rod has all the right stuff, including a finned Buick brake drum.

5

5 This Buick finned drum is actually a reproduction piece made of aluminum. Offered by So-Cal Speed Shop, it slips over the disc brake rotor so it resembles the early Ford brakes.

6 Chromed backing plates help dress up the car's front end. In fact, chrome on most of the steering components helps, too!

7 Hydraulic, or juice, brakes were added to the rear of the early hot rods, too. Notice that the rear tire on this Model A is an Indy Firestone.

6

7

8   Some hot rodders will tell you that "if it don't go, then chrome it." In the case of this car's brakes, that adage really is true.

9   You can see the disc brake rotor and caliper behind the spokes of this new-generation American Racing Torq-Thrust wheel.

Drivetrains:
Wheels and Tires

Most of us remember the children's song from grade school that contains the verse, "the wheels on the bus go 'round and 'round." When those wheels stop rolling, though, their details and highlights become visible for all the world to see. Same goes for the tires, which are wrapped 'round those wheels that go 'round and 'round. It's at that point, when the car stops, that an experienced hot rod builder or enthusiast will agree that the right set of wheels and tires can make the car.

Wheels and tires should also be in harmony with the car's theme. Since this book addresses primarily traditional hot rods, it makes little sense to consider using 20-inch billet wheels with low-profile rubber-band tires. Conversely, a set of original Ford solid wheels with 6.00x16 bias-ply tires on a high-tech roadster would look silly.

As you build your car, take time to think about the wheels and tires you'll eventually place under it. Since they are among the last components you'll put on the car, there's no excuse for not planning for them. So, let the wheels inside your head go 'round and 'round while you consider the best set of wheels and tires for your hot rod project.

2   Before you buy your wheels, determine the proper amount of back space for the fronts and rears. An experienced salesman can help you here. This hot rod has 3½ inches of back spacing for its American wheels.

3   If your car's theme favors high performance, the correct tires will help convey the message. This "cheater" slick, so named because it has two tread grooves to make it street legal, is from M&H Racemaster.

4   Reversed rims are a good way to fill those wheelwells with steel and rubber. The deep-set baby moon caps and stainless-steel trim rings give added definition to the wheel on this 1957 Oldsmobile.

5

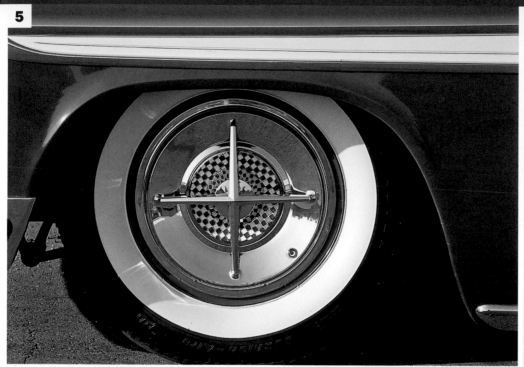

6

7

8

5 Four-spoke wheel covers from late-1950s Dodge Lancers are popular for a traditional custom car look. It took a lot of time and patience to paint the checkered pattern in this wheel cover's center section.

6 Halibrand is a name that etched its place in racing and hot rod lore back in 1947. This wheel is a replica of Ted Halibrand's Sprint wheel, so named because it was originally developed for oval-track sprint race cars.

7 Here's a good way to mix traditional styling with current tire technology. This early wire wheel with 1932 Ford center cap is wrapped with a wide whitewall radial tire offered by Coker Tire, a company that specializes in vintage tires.

8 Recently the word "patina" has become popular among traditional hot rod enthusiasts. You won't find much more patina than what's on Ed Iskenderian's wheels. These wide whitewall tires show their age, but they still look cool!

9   This 19-inch Buffalo wire wheel was favored by hot rodders during the prewar era of the 1930s. Many race cars of that time used Buffalo wheels for their light weight and strength.

10   A trick practiced by early hot rodders was to upgrade their Ford Model T wheels with something newer. In this case, a 1926 T is equipped with 1932 Plymouth wheels with chromed center caps.

11   Another lesson in style is served up by Lil' John Buttera. The wire-spoke wheels convey a sense of traditional styling, but behind the chrome you catch a glimpse of the disc brakes, which were avant-garde when this car was built during the 1970s.

12   More attention to styling theme can be seen here. The deep-set wire wheel has a tire with an aggressive tread pattern, much like what you'd see for a dirt-track race car. This red roadster resembles a modified track racer.

13   Nothing fancy here, just a 14-inch Ford wheel dressed with a 1946 Ford cap and ring, then wrapped with a Firestone wide whitewall tire. I like the way the salt crystals from the Bonneville Salt Flats stick to the rubber!

14   Another deep-set Ford solid wheel with a center cap and rim ring shows how clean this design can be. In this case, the wheel is painted the same color as the car, although it's popular to contrast the two.

15 Don't want to pay to have those aluminum wheels polished? Or maybe you don't want to deal with keeping them shiny. Here's a way out of both: just paint them to match your hot rod's body color coat.

16 The blood red paint gives this Kelsey Hayes wheel a truly vintage look. It also helps that it's wrapped with a tractor-style Firestone tire. These ribbed tires were used on oval-track racecars back in the 1940s and 1950s.

17 You can't go wrong with any five-spoke wheel that resembles American Racing's original Torq-Thrust design, introduced during the 1960s. It's popular today to polish or chrome those five-spokers.

18 You really can't get any more traditional than this combination on the Doane Spencer 1932 Ford roadster. This is a standard-width Ford wheel, dressed with the same ware Spencer used back in the 1950s when he built the highboy.

19

19 Another example of mixing today's technology—that's the wide whitewall radial tire—with a Ford solid wheel. Dress it with an early-style center cap and rim ring, and you've got a traditional-style wheel/tire combo that performs well.

20 Chrome wheels were especially popular back in the 1960s, when this 1932 Ford coupe was transformed into a hot rod. Notice the extra attention that was given to the tires, highlighting the name and specs with paint. This, too, was popular in the 1960s.

21 A good example of contrasting colors is seen here. The pale yellow wheels emphasize the car's blue paint. Look closer, though, and you will see yet another color—red on the pinstripes around the center cap and red in the Ford script.

22 This is about as brash as you can be with a hot rod. This T-bucket rides on M&H Racemaster slicks. Notice the subtle pinstriping on the wheel's rim; the added color helps break up the red.

20

21

22

23 Another example of a Halibrand magnesium wheel, except it's a replica from Wheel Vintiques and it's made of aluminum. According to Halibrand records, this design was originally intended for use on oval-track midget racers.

24 The chrome wheels on the *American Graffiti* coupe are probably the most recognizable wheels in all of hot rodding. According to Rick Figari, the car's current owner, they are the same wheels it has had since the movie was filmed.

25 This Halibrand replica is a wheel that was originally marketed as a front wheel for dragsters and sprint cars. Made by PS Engineering, it resides on a 1931 Plymouth roadster.

26   Mooneyes wheel covers are classics. Developed by Dean Moon, the idea was to help streamline the wheels for Bonneville and drag racing. The covers are made of spun aluminum and are attached to the wheel by using three sheetmetal screws.

27   Another wheel cover favored by the custom car crowd is the tri-spinner cover originally found on the Oldsmobile Fiesta in the 1950s. Reproduction covers are available on the aftermarket.

28   The same, only different: This Olds Fiesta wheel cover has the iconic globe emblem on each of the three spinners, plus the center section's graphics have a checkerboard pattern.

29   Dare to be different. Even though this wheel is on a 1929 Ford, the hubcaps are from a Mercury. One way to dress up wheels is to include pinstripes and accent paint, as seen on this wheel assembly.

30 Okay, it's not the cleanest wheel-and-tire combination on the block, but its funk makes you look twice. The red accent color seems to give the car's gray primer coat a little more purpose.

31 Another primer helper can be seen here. The wheel cover got a small dose of red paint and a nose cone in the center, and a touch of flat white paint inside the wheelwell helps brighten up the otherwise dull gray primer coat.

32 This reversed offset wheel is tastefully done. Give the wheel a dash of red paint, press on the 1949 Ford hubcap, then wrap a bias-ply wide whitewall tire around it, and you've got an instant classic for your hot rod.

33 Who says all traditional hot rods with steelie wheels have to have those center hoops painted bright red? Painting the wheels a subtle color, such as gray, sometimes can have the same double-take effect.

RACER'S EDGE

Hot rodders often misuse the phrase "mag wheel," by referring to a wheel that's made of cast aluminum or, more recently, forged or billet aluminum. The phrase "mag wheel" actually traces back to the racetracks of America where savvy car builders utilized the lightweight, yet strong, properties of cast magnesium to construct the wheels for their cars. Clearly, it was through racing on Southern California's alkaline dry lakes, Bonneville's pristine white Salt Flats, or the rough and gritty dirt-surface oval tracks of America that the builders learned a lot about engineering lighter, stronger, and all-around better wheels and tires for their cars.

The sport of hot rodding was born on the dry lakes and at Bonneville. Many of the wheel designs seen on the street today can trace their origins to these dry lakes and closed-circuit tracks across America.

You can still find original racing wheels and tires at automotive swap meets. I photographed this ensemble at the 1995 NHRA California Hot Rod Reunion. I found it interesting that the old and cracked Pirelli tires matched.

When hot rodders discovered quarter-mile drag racing, hot rodding soared to new heights. Nationally sanctioned events also served as marketing sources for wheel and tire manufacturers to sell their wares.

Original Halibrand race wheels were made of cast magnesium, a metal known for its strength and light weight. Thus was born the phrase "mag wheel," short for magnesium wheel.

Among the more popular nostalgic wheels are the five-spoke American Racing Torq-Thrusts, introduced during the 1960s. They were available in cast aluminum or, like this wheel, magnesium.

Shopping at automotive swap meets will net you some interesting parts, such as the dished magnesium wheel on the back of this 1932 Ford roadster. This is an 18-inch wheel-and-tire combination.

Magnesium is extremely sensitive to oxidation, making mag wheels hard to keep polished. The owner of this 1932 Ford roadster polishes his Halibrands every week. This wheel is a 12x16-inch wrapped with a Goodyear racing tire.

Paint and Graphics
Fancy Colors

Selecting the right paint and graphics for your hot rod is probably one of the toughest challenges you'll face with your project. Get the color right, and your project will have a happy ending. Choose the wrong color and graphics, and you risk having all of your hard work look like . . . well, you get the picture.

Indeed, paint and graphics are so important that many books have been written on these subjects. So rather than even bother talking about the dos and don'ts of what makes a good paint job, we'll instead use our time to look at

some of the basic elements of design and style.

For a more complete understanding, I suggest you buy JoAnn Bortles' *Custom Painting Idea Book*, available from Motorbooks. JoAnn is an experienced painter with plenty of knowledge about the art, and her book addresses the fundamentals that every hot rod builder should know about paint and graphics. In the meantime, we'll spend the next few pages acquainting ourselves with what I consider to be some unique and tasteful paint jobs for traditional-style hot rods and customs.

2 Dare to be different. If you want to use some really wild graphics, decoupage the paint with pages from old hot rod magazines.

3 The flames on this 1934 Ford coupe seem to flow smoothly over the signature-series fenders and hood.

4 If you have a barn find like this Deuce highboy, you might consider leaving the old paint, capturing its patina in the process.

5

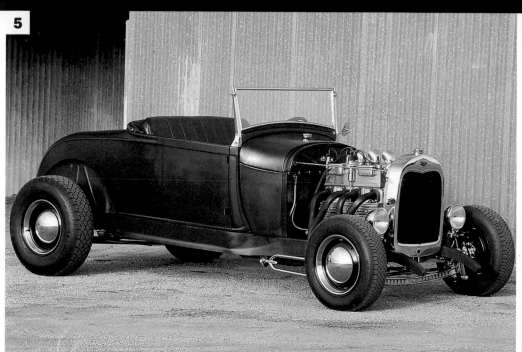

5   Primer finishes are popular today. Not only are they easy to apply, but they also require little upkeep in terms of waxing.

6   Scallops were especially popular on open-wheel race cars during the 1930s, and this Ford pickup truck proves why.

7   A reverse-flame pattern, as on this 1936 Ford phaeton, looks cool and teases the eye in the process.

8   The V-8 graphics on this fenderless 1933 Ford were inspired by Ford's Indianapolis 500 effort of 1935.

6

7

8

9 This 1960 Buick is drenched with scallop graphics that are reminiscent of what customizer Larry Watson did half a century ago.

10 Primer finishes are dull in color, but they don't have to be dull in appearance. Bright flames liven up this 1937 Chevrolet's primer.

11 Gray primer, accented with bright red wheels and shiny new chrome, make this turtleback Ford stand out.

12 These flowing scallop flames were applied using a $5 can of aerosol red paint.

13 What began as a rather plain-looking 1951 Chevrolet now rides the road wearing bold traditional flames on the front.

14 A quick coat of gloss white paint dressed with pinstripe flames gives this old Ford its own look.

15 The sheet metal on this 1950 Lincoln was turned into a painter's pallet for flames and miscellaneous graphics.

16 Bright red paint and a touch of Von Dutch–style pinstripes make for an eye-catching 1932 Ford highboy.

17 A slight chop to the top and a low riding stance are just the ticket for the racer-like scallops on this Model A sedan.

18 The red shadowing along the white scallops helps liven up an otherwise plain color.

19 Custom-car owners have always been fond of naming their cars. The placement of the name helps balance out the graphics on this 1955 Chevrolet.

20 The car-length flames on this 1940 Ford sedan help break up the monotony of its smooth sheet metal.

21

21 Use the body's curves and features to accent the flames. This Deuce roadster's flames seem to lap out of the hood's side louvers.

22 Three-dimensional graphics aren't easy to apply, but when they're done right, they look oh-so right!

23 Chroming the headlight buckets helps amplify the effect that the graphics have on this hot rod.

24 Pale metallic blue isn't a popular color, but this Deuce highboy wears it well, thanks to traditional-style flames.

22

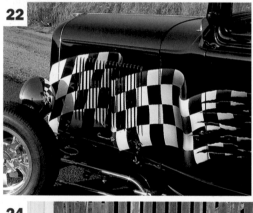

23

24

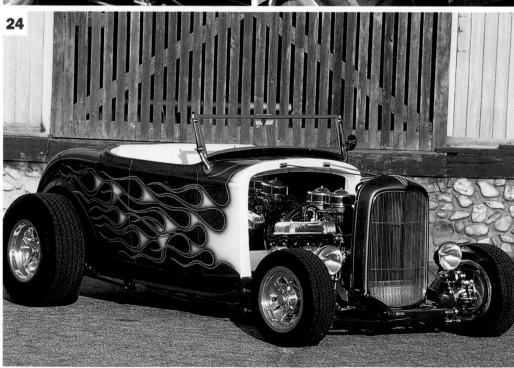

25   The origin of candy colors is credited to Joe Bailon. This Candy Apple Red was applied back in the early 1960s, and it still looked fresh when I photographed it in 1991.

26   Nothing special here, just one really fine black paint job that was hand-rubbed to a deep luster.

27   Most car builders shy away from white because it lacks depth, but this 1959 Ford Ranchero wears its original Colonial White color rather well, don't you think?

28   This magenta paint job probably would have flopped if it weren't for the yellow beltline stripe and Offy Special nose art.

29

30

31

29 Retaining the original trim and nameplates sometimes gives a hot rod its own eloquent theme.

30 You can take two subtle colors—mint green and cream white—and make them shout just by adding color to the wheels.

31 Painting a big 1950s-era doorslammer black can be a challenge. This one passes the acid test—no waves or ripples show.

32   The massive pale yellow front would look boring on this 1940 Ford if it weren't for the pinstripes around the hood spear.

33   Liven up your car's paint job with some funky artwork. The woodpecker has always been a favorite among rodders.

34   The South shall rise again! I had to perch myself on a wall to capture the stars-and-bars graphics on the top of this sedan.

35   Contrasting colors, such as the red solid wheels against the pale yellow flames, work well with a dark base color.

36   Another example of good placement of the car name is seen on this 1958 Chevrolet's side window.

37 Flames licking down the sides of this Buick distract your eye so that you really don't notice that this is a four-door!

38 Red can usually stand on its own merits, but there's nothing wrong with torching it with some flames.

39 Years ago, blue dots in the taillights were outlawed in most states. Today's laws are less strict, allowing this nostalgic style to come back.

40 I liked the way the sunset played on this 1937 Ford's front fender, so I shot this photograph. As one of my mentors, Tex Smith, was fond of saying: 'nuff said.

41   The Colorado sunset is reflected in this Model A's hood. This is the time of day when a good black paint job really stands out.

42   Sometimes less is more, and in this case, less chrome in the engine bay is more feast for the eyes, thanks to some red paint.

43   Subtle hood graphics help give this black paint job its rich, deep color.

44   Brass on the radiator and white paint on the firewall and on the hood's underbelly make you feel as though you're back in the 1950s.

PINSTRIPES

I love pinstripes on a hot rod. They're artful and colorful, and strategically placed pinstripes can distract the eye from the rest of the car's style elements. That way, whoever checks out your car is treated to essentially two shows in one; the car is the star, but those thin stripes warrant second billing.

Pinstripes can consist of only a few well-placed lines or a swirl of motion left by the striper's horsehair brush. Sometimes pinstripers will tell a story within their designs, while others simply lay one line and then carry on to the next stripe. Pinstripes can accent a particular feature on a car, or they can stand alone to boldly proclaim that "this is art"—it's art on the side of a hot rod. No matter the intent, pinstripes add color and depth to a car's paint, so every hot rod builder should at least consider their applications.

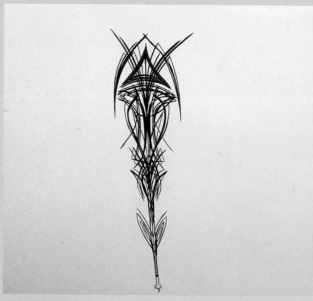

It takes a skilled and steady hand to apply a gaggle of pinstripes like this. Using multiple colors adds to its artful charm.

A few simple, yet strategic, swipes with the horsehair brush, and suddenly this 1932 Ford's door handle takes on new meaning.

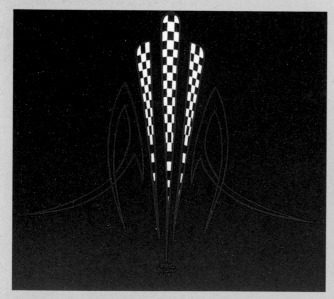

These pinstripes contain their own graphics. The pinstriper also used the occasion to sign his work.

The graphics-within-the-pinstripes theme plays out at the front of this hot rod as well.

The chrome on this 1954 Chevrolet was pretty tired, but the car's owner livened up the party with some colorful stripes.

The editors at *Street Rodder* magazine built this replica of Tom McMullen's famous Deuce roadster, stripes and all. Who said editorz can't spell?

Again, contrasting colors work to make a statement. The coral color on this 1957 Oldsmobile gains masculinity thanks to the stripes.

An old radiator grille and shell take on new life when a few red and white pinstripes are applied.

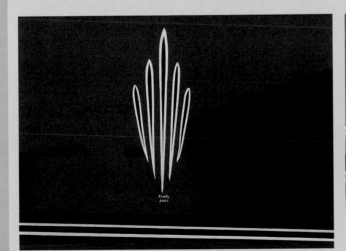

Shaky Jake was one of the popular pinstripers of the 1970s and 1980s. You can see his signature on this pinstripe job.

The soft lavender stripes on this Ford's radiator shell help direct the eye back to the car's black paint job.

Paint and Graphics
Before and After

Throughout this book, you have been given more than a few ideas for your hot rod project. Now the question arises: Where should you begin with your project? Well, how about at the beginning? It's going to require some careful planning on your part and a lot of hard work, not to mention more than a few dollars. As you've seen in the previous pages, though, it can be done and can be well worth it. As a final pep talk, I've included some before-and-after photos of a few hot rods that I had the opportunity to photograph from beginning to end. Never forget—there is light at the end of the tunnel.

1 Swap meets and car-for-sale corrals are always good places to start when shopping for a hot rod project. The worst thing you can do is to purchase your car on an impulse.

2 Before: This 1936 Ford pickup belongs to Tom Leonardo. He used the old hauler as his parts chaser for years, calling the dingy Ford "Old Faithful."

3 After: Hey, Old Faithful cleans up pretty good! Tom spent less than a year chasing parts for his old parts chaser to end up with this diamond in the rough.

4

5

6

7

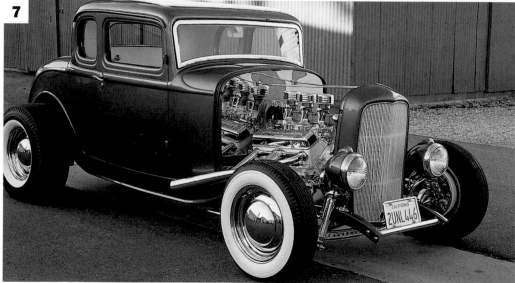

4 Before: Chuck DeHaras has commissioned the So-Cal Speed Shop to build several of his hot rods. This was the first, an extended-cab Model A pickup.

5 After: That's Chuck behind the wheel during the truck's shakedown run. This was a rather extensive project, and So-Cal's Pete Chapouris allowed me to cover it from start to finish.

6 Before: Here's another project from my good friend Tom Leonardo. To help sort the car's mechanicals, Tom made it a driver with primer paint.

7 After: Curious about what a fresh paint job with chrome trim, new interior, and different wheels can do? This car was featured in *Rod & Custom* magazine.

Index

Other **Motorbooks** titles of interest:

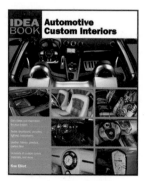

**AUTOMOTIVE
CUSTOM INTERIORS**
ISBN 978-0-7603-3288-7

CUSTOM PAINTING
ISBN 978-0-7603-3169-9

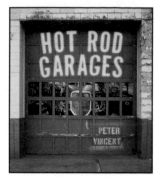

HOT ROD GARAGES
ISBN 978-0-7603-2696-1

**HOW TO PAINT
YOUR SHOW CAR**
ISBN 978-0-7603-3275-7

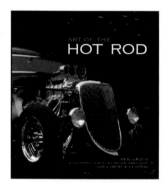

**ART OF THE
HOT ROD**
ISBN 978-0-7603-2282-6

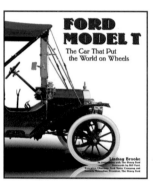

FORD MODEL T
ISBN 978-0-7603-2728-9

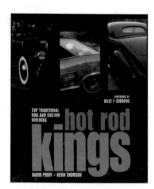

HOT ROD KINGS
ISBN 978-0-7603-2738-8

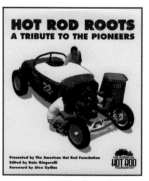

HOT ROD ROOTS
ISBN 978-0-7603-2818-7

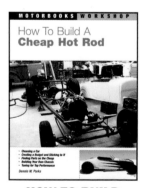

**HOW TO BUILD
A CHEAP HOT ROD**
ISBN 978-0-7603-2348-9

motorbooks

Find us on the internet at **www.motorbooks.com**